Middle of the Lake

The Fed-Up Enablers' Guide to Constructive Love

Written by Frank K

Illustrated by Holly West

BEARHEAD PUBLISHING
-BhP-
Brandenburg, Kentucky
www.bearheadpublishing.com

Middle of the Lake
The Fed Up Enablers' Guide to Constructive Love
by Frank K

Illustrations by Holly West

Cover Design by Bearhead Publishing

First Printing - August 2019

ISBN: 978-1-937508-62-3
1 2 3 4 5 6 7 8 9

Proudly printed in the United States of America.

Middle of the Lake

The Fed-Up Enablers' Guide to Constructive Love

Middle of the Lake

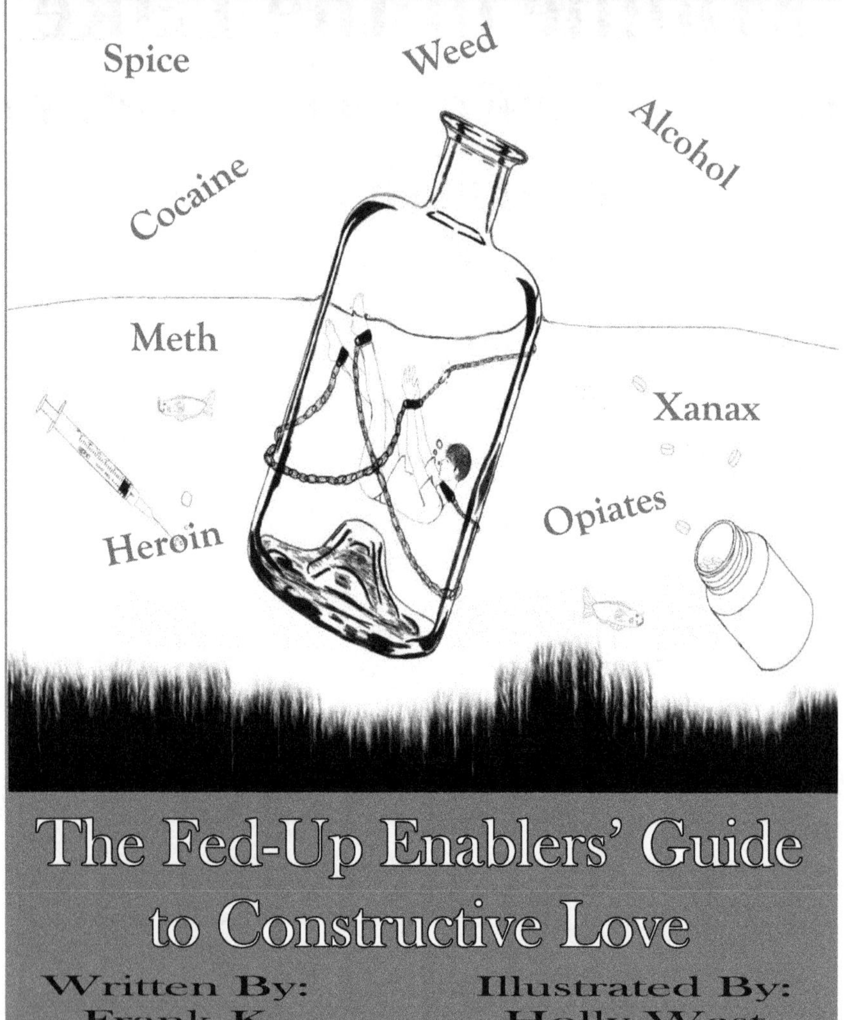

The Fed-Up Enablers' Guide to Constructive Love

Written By:
Frank K

Illustrated By:
Holly West

Dedication

This book is dedicated to all who suffer from the diseases of alcoholism and addiction and to all the family members and friends who have suffered as a result of these deadly diseases.

Acknowledgments

I would like to give thanks to my beautiful bride Theresa for standing by me during my journey to sobriety and supporting my quest to help the next alcoholic and addict to get this wonderful gift of freedom. Special thanks to my six lovely children. Thanks to my worldwide recovery family for the amazing fellowship. Deep thanks to Misty West for suggesting Holly to illustrate this book. Finally, thanks to Holly West for the incredible illustrations that brought this book to life.

Get Ready

Join me in a journey into a topic and term that is thrown around in a reckless manner. It is a term that has become popular when discussing the devastating crisis of alcoholism and addiction of the addict, the alcoholic and their families. The term is ENABLE or ENABLING. How many parents and loved ones who are struggling to somehow, someway, save their son, daughter, mother, father, or sibling, get this short and cold advice "Stop enabling him or her. Use tough love. Cut them off"? I do not totally disagree with this advice, but to the parent who is watching their child literally die in front of them, this advice, although somewhat logical, is incomplete, shortsighted, and goes against every natural instinct a parent or loved one has. Unfortunately, dealing with someone who is in the grips of addiction of any sort is not that simple. Each situation, addicted person, and the family dynamic is unique, confusing, and heartbreaking and cannot ever be treated with a cookie cutter solution. This is a painful situation and I feel your pain.

This book is an attempt to look at the crisis of alcoholism and addiction from both the alcoholic's and addict's view and from the parents, husbands, wives, sons, daughters, and loved ones who unintentionally are caught up in the fall-out of the addict's behavior. From this point forward when I use the term addict, it also includes the alcoholic because alcohol is a drug and the alcoholic's drug of choice is alcohol. In addition, many addicts are cross-addicted to both alcohol and drugs.

We will explore the brutal truth that addiction is not an individual struggle, it affects every life the addict touches. The addict, unchecked, will not only destroy their life but also the lives the addict touches. We will dissect the disease concept of addiction to best understand the addict and the disease they struggle with. We will take a deep dive into what a loved one can do to help the addict without actually hurting them and themselves in the process. We will look at how some desperate attempts to save the addict are fruitless and destroy the loving person and the families attempting to help.

We will examine the effect the addict has on family relationships and how disagreements and arguments between family members on what to do and how to help the addict can rip families and marriages apart. Yes, addiction is a family disease, not a spectator sport; everyone who is in contact with the addict is on the field and gets to play whether they want to or not. We will dissect the meaning of the buzzword enabling and put the term in perspective and practical application.

Embedded in this book is a short graphic novel, which I wrote and is beautifully and skillfully illustrated by Holly West, an amazingly talented fifteen-year-old high school student. I wrote the short story - the basis for the graphic novel - ten years prior to writing this book. The story is about someone I care deeply for and desperately tried to help. I was at a point where every attempt to help this addict backfired. Although the assistance my wife and I gave to our addict provided some immediate relief, the addiction and the devastating effects on the addict and the family worsened. In my case, the conflict between the desperate desire to save the addict from jail and death and the futility of my efforts resulted in anger, fear, resentment, argument, and misery for all. The addict and my entire family got steadily sicker and never better.

Some of you are probably saying, “HOLD ON THERE! I do not see a PHD or an MD behind your name on the cover of this book. Why should I take this journey with you? What qualifications do you have to write a book about such an important subject?” Well, I write this book from two perspectives.

The first is the school of hard knocks. I am the parent of an addict who has struggled with this issue for over a decade, and I continue to struggle with the subject of enabling today. I am also a recovered alcoholic with over eight and half years of unbroken sobriety as I write these words.

Secondly, I have made it my avocation to reach out and help other alcoholics and addicts find sobriety. I work with sufferers on a daily basis giving them the tools to find happiness and lasting sobriety. I chair meetings for groups, speak throughout the community, and bring the message of hope into the local prisons. I have spent countless hours talking and working with family members explaining the disease their loved ones have and helping them negotiate these treacherous and heartbreaking waters. I have also written two other books on the subjects of alcoholism and addiction. Therefore, my qualifications have not come from a classroom but from real life experience.

Are you still with me?

Get Set

Before we journey into the graphic novel section, let us take an introductory look at the term "enabling". Enabling or to enable is not necessarily a bad thing to do. Webster's defines the word enable as, a: to provide with the means or opportunity; b: to make possible, practical, or easy. It would appear from the definition that enabling is a very good thing and it certainly can be. Good parents do positive enabling all the time. Certainly, it is natural and in fact almost necessary to give your child a boost or encouragement to get ahead in life. We want our children and our family to have a great and productive life.

Imagine your nine-year-old daughter comes home from school with a note from the teacher. The note states that their daughter is excelling in music class and has a natural talent for the piano. The note goes on to suggest that parents foster this emerging talent. Wow, this is amazing news for any parent. The parents, excited and proud, talk to their daughter and their daughter expresses her excitement about mastering the piano. Their daughter is glowing with excitement and cannot stop talking about the song she learned on the piano. The parents, in a gesture of positive and loving enabling, and despite a limited income and savings account, purchase a two thousand dollar piano and pay for weekly lessons for their daughter. This example is played out all over the world with talents such as sports, academics, and the arts. Parents gifting newlyweds with the means to lessen the cost of starting out on their own is done all the time. Helping loved ones over and through life's little roadblocks is how families help each other.

Eleven years later the same daughter, now twenty and in a prestigious school for the musical arts, comes to her parents frightened and upset. She states that she is failing out of school and is addicted to heroin and begs her parents for help. The parents are shocked, surprised, and scared. She, of course, can't afford treatment. The parents decide to negotiate a semester off from school and pay five thousand dollars to place their daughter into the best drug rehabilitation center in the area. According to the definition, this, too, is positive enabling. They are providing their daughter the opportunity to get clean and continue her career and life's ambition.

In both cases, the parents have made a financial sacrifice for the well-being and future of their daughter. First, investing in the piano and the lessons and second helping her get off the drugs. If she recovers from the drug addiction, finishes school, and has a wonderful music career then the parents have succeeded. Everyone lives happily ever after. Unfortunately, this example of successful enabling when it comes to addiction is the exception and not the common outcome.

Story after story I have heard, and experienced myself, goes generally like this. The daughter completes her rehabilitation feeling great, sorry for her mistake, and grateful for the opportunity her parents gave her. She does not intend to ever touch a drug again. She thinks to herself, *no one in her right mind would ever go down that path again.* She confidently states she has the problem licked and will never make that stupid mistake again! She returns to school and excels for a semester. The parents breathe a sigh of relief and are happy their daughter is back on track. They feel they have diverted a disaster and are confident she would never mess with drugs again.

After a semester, the daughter relapses and crashes her car into another parked car. The result is a DUI and she is expelled from school. The parents pay a lawyer to prevent jail time and pay to put their daughter back into a rehabilitation center. This time the total bill is over fifteen thousand dollars. As with the first stay in the rehabilitation center, the daughter comes out healthy and ready to fulfill her goals. The parents again relieved, agree to enroll her into a lesser but still acceptable music program. At this point, they can barely afford that. She needs transportation and since she cannot afford to replace the car she wrecked, they purchase her a used car. The parents have now laid out over twenty five thousand dollars to enable their daughter to get on track. They have put off work on their home, a long planned second honeymoon, and are swimming in debt. At this point, they are concerned, but their daughter is their number one priority!

Over the next ten years, the relapses come often and with greater consequences. Between relapses, the parents see glimmers of the daughter with all that potential they saw at a young age. The father continues to support their daughter in every conceivable way possible to include putting a second mortgage on the house and delaying retirement. The mother quickly grows tired of sacrificing everything for their daughter. She feels that their daughter is lying about her commitment to get off the drugs and has caught her in many lies over the years. This causes a great rift in the marriage. In fact, this once happy marriage and family is now totally consumed with the addiction of the daughter.

Finally, the stress causes the parents to separate and divorce. The daughter, knowing her mother would no longer help her, continues to seek and get constant financial help from the father who is now bankrupt and living in a small apartment. The daughter finally overdoses and dies at age 39. She left in her wake a path of destruction that destroyed her parents. Both parents died heartbroken, penniless, and lonely.

You may think the father to be a hero, he gave up is entire life for his daughter. However, no matter how many times he bailed her out and set her back on her feet she got worse, never better. What went wrong? It certainly was not a lack of love or support. The question is when did the positive enabling become negative enabling? When was it time for the parents to stop taking their daughter's consequences upon themselves and let their daughter face them herself? Did the fact that the daughter always had a safety net and never had to fully bear the consequences of her actions keep her from breaking the addiction? Were the parents unknowingly contributing to the addiction that killed their daughter?

We will examine these questions.

Let's Go!

The short graphic novel we are about to read is to give us food for thought. Hopefully the example of our young piano prodigy on the previous page has already started you thinking. I sat down and wrote this story we are about to experience approximately ten years ago. I was a distraught parent struggling with how to help our child who was struggling with a drug addiction. The addiction was not only tearing our child apart, but it was tearing our marriage apart. We were placing all our focus on one child and beginning to neglect the other five children. Money was invested and wasted, time off work was taken, and arguments were happening between my wife and me, we were becoming as sick as the child we were trying to help.

It was also the first time I started to look at my alcoholism. My drinking was an issue that I refused to deal with. This reflective short story may have been the seed to my journey from an active alcoholic to a recovered alcoholic. Within two years of writing this story, I began my journey into sobriety.

As you read the story, try to put yourself in all three characters shoes. Attempt to place all preconceived notions aside and flow with the story. Try not to look for the differences in your personal experiences, rather look for the similarities. The story will have four possible endings. There is no prize for picking a winning or correct ending.

After the story, the remainder of the book will examine all the questions posed in the previous pages. There will be no preaching; no judgment; no magic pill; just an honest look at the issue of enabling from as many angles as possible. I hope to give understanding, techniques, and suggestions from my experience that may help guide your thoughts, plans, and actions when dealing with someone close to you that is suffering from addiction to drugs, alcohol, or both.

Turn the page with me and enter the world of

The Boy in the Middle of the Lake

The Boy in the Middle of the Lake

A beautiful boy was born to two good and loving parents.

They raised him well, taught him manners and the importance of hard work and education.

One day the mother saw the young boy standing by the edge of the lake and staring out at the middle.

The mother, very concerned, took the opportunity to warn her son never to swim out to the middle of the lake because he could drown.

All was well.

The boy grew and became a young man.

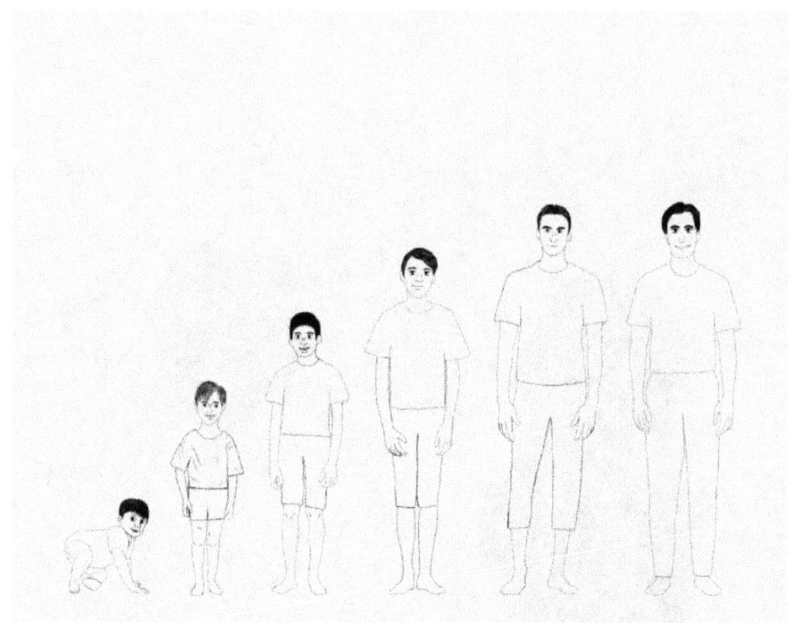

The parents were proud of their son.

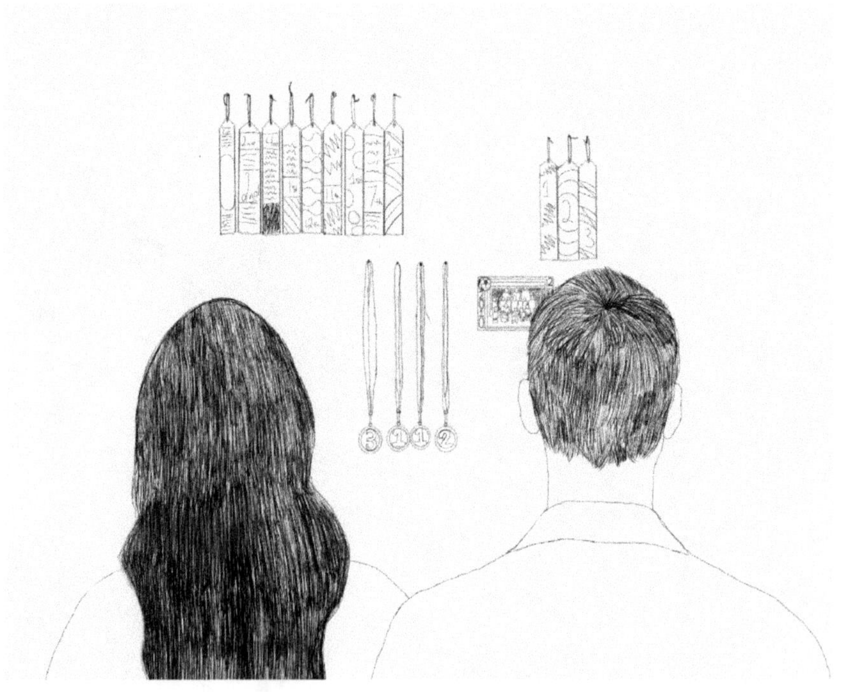

He did well in school.

He made lots of friends and was popular.

One beautiful spring day the strapping young man now twenty was standing by the edge of the lake.

He remembered what his mother told him, but he was now a man and thought he could handle anything.

He took off his shoes and shirt and dove in and started swimming towards the middle of the lake.

When he arrived at the middle of the lake, an incredible euphoria came over him. It was the most wonderful feeling he ever felt.

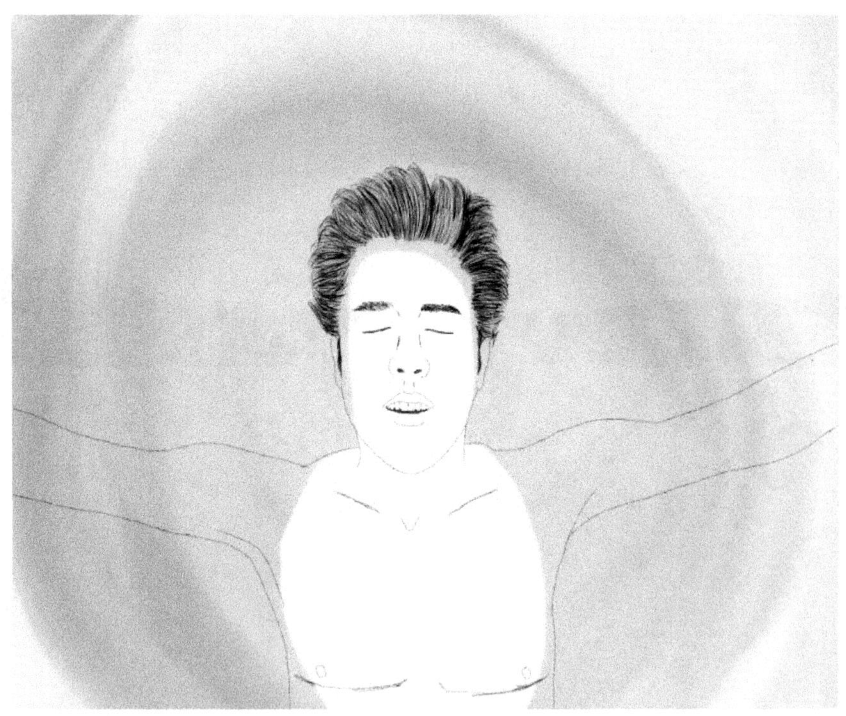

After a while, he remembered his mother's warning and swam back to shore.

A week went by, the man was walking by the lake, and he remembered how incredible it felt in the middle of the lake.

He also thought of his mother's warning. However, he went out there last week and got back safely. He is a man now and can handle the lake.

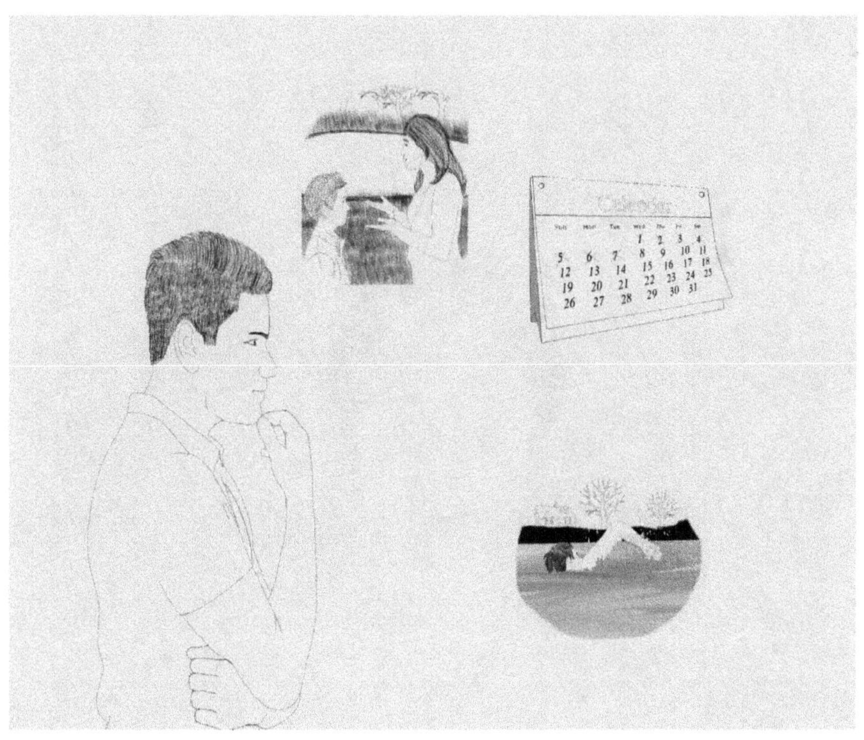

So, he swam out again and the feeling was just as amazing as last time.

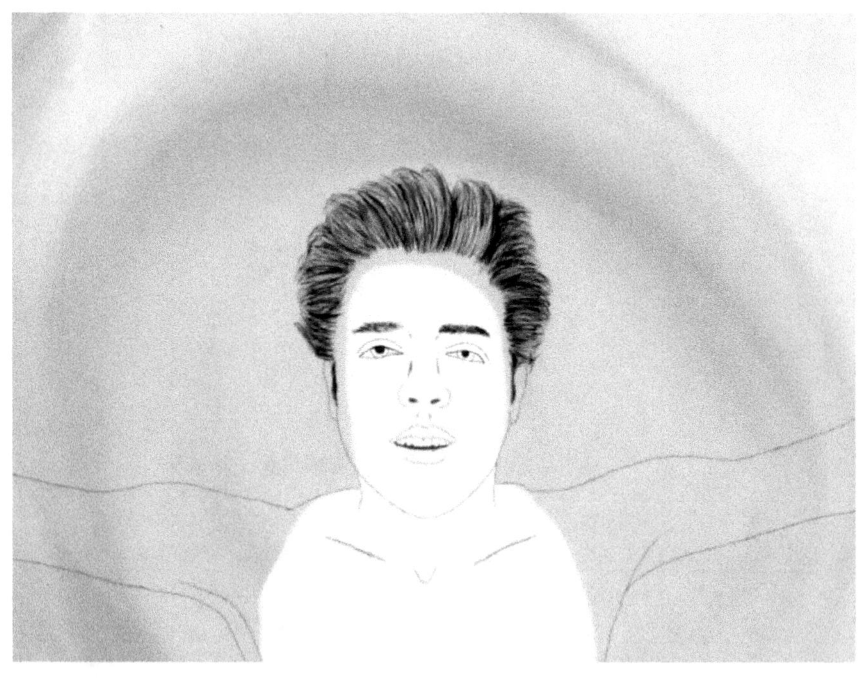

He stayed longer but was worried his parents would find out and he swam back to shore.

Over the next month, he would swim out to the middle of the lake once a week.

A few weeks later, he would swim out a couple times a week. Not too shortly after that, he would go every night.

The middle of the lake felt so good. His parents did not know. He worked the family farm during the day. He told himself he could handle this.

His grades began to slip at school. All he could think about was being in the middle of the lake.

He did not have time for his friends and activities.

One weekend the family visited close cousins a town over for a short two-day visit.

The young man knew he would miss the lake but also knew it was only a few days.

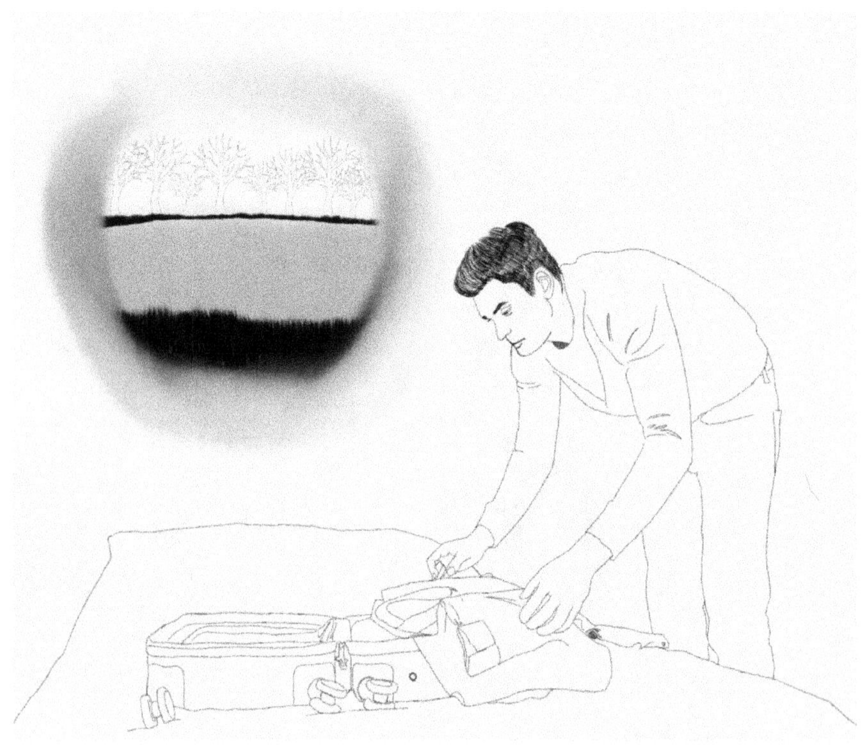

On a warm, sunny day, the family left for their trip. The boy was looking forward to seeing his cousins.

However, a strange thing happened that night. He started to feel sick. The feeling got worse as the night went on.

He told his parents he did not feel well and went home early.

When he arrived home, he swam back out to the middle of the lake and to his surprise the mysterious sickness went away.

The boy didn't realize his sickness was directly related to him being away from the lake.

Over time, he spent more and more time in the middle of the lake. In fact, if he were out of the lake for more than a few hours he would get sick.

He began to realize he was swimming out to the middle of the lake not to get that wonderful feeling anymore but actually to not feel sick.

Nothing mattered to him but the middle of the lake.

He started ignoring his responsibilities on the farm and lost interest in his family.

His parents noticed the change in his behavior and got worried.

They questioned him in an effort to figure this change out.

The young man denied that there was any problem.

One evening the mother, so concerned about her son, followed him to the lake.

She was shocked and horrified when she saw him swim out to the middle of the lake.

She called out to him to swim back.

Now that his secret was out and knowing his mother was right, he embarrassingly swam to shore and promised his mother he would never go into the lake again.

She reminded him how dangerous the middle of the lake was.

The young man knew his mother was right and made a promise to himself he would stay out of the lake.

But, after a very short period of time he began to feel sick again.

He tried to fight off the feeling but all he could think of was getting back to the lake.

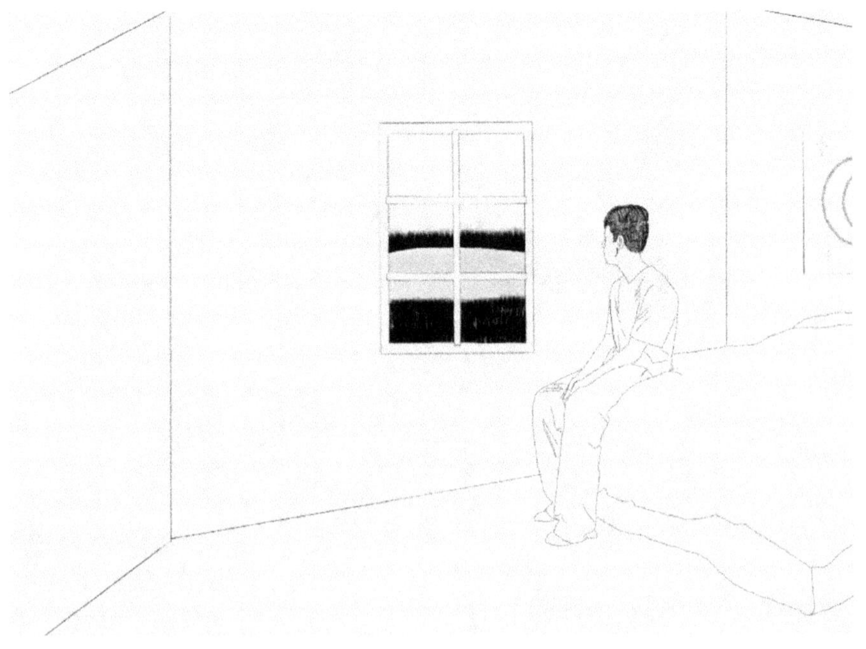

Finally, sick and in pain, he stumbled down to the lake and swam out.

He immediately felt better and just stayed in the middle of the lake floating and treading water.

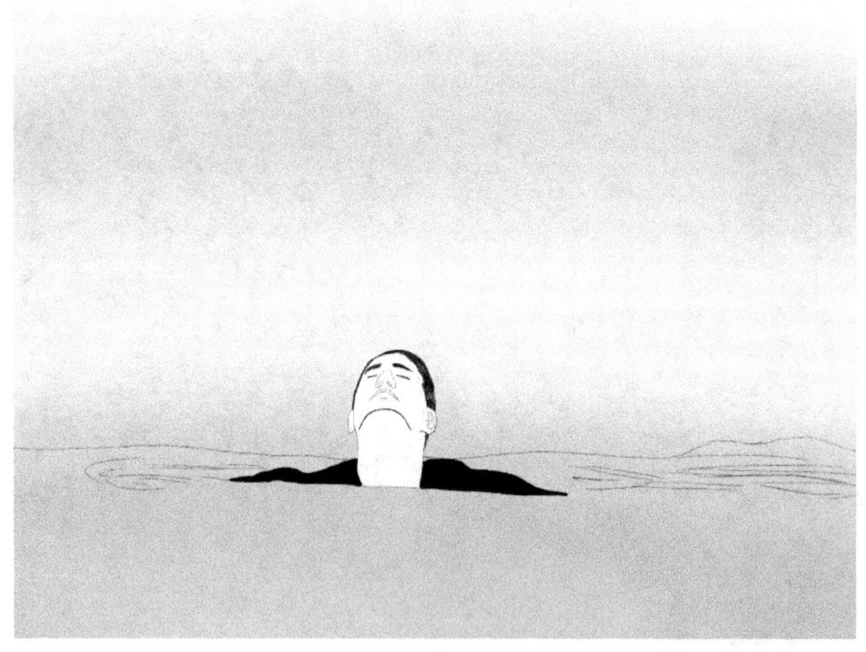

His parents notice the boy missing and went to find him.

His parents stood by the edge of the lake calling out to him to swim back. He ignored their calls.

He was content and only cared about being in the middle of the lake.

His parents stayed by the shore pleading and worrying all night long.

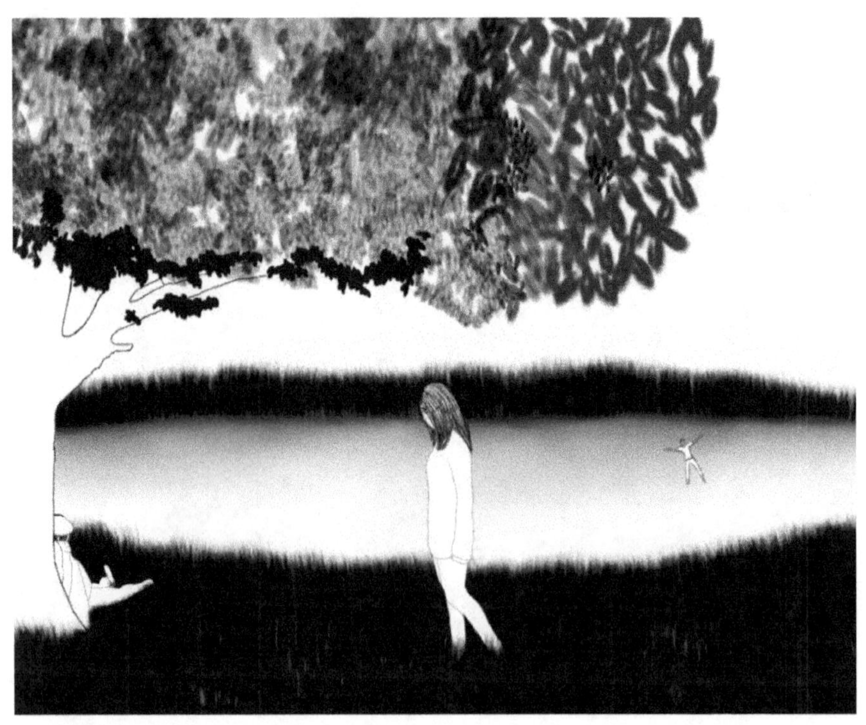

At dawn, the young man grew tired. He began to sink to the bottom of the lake.

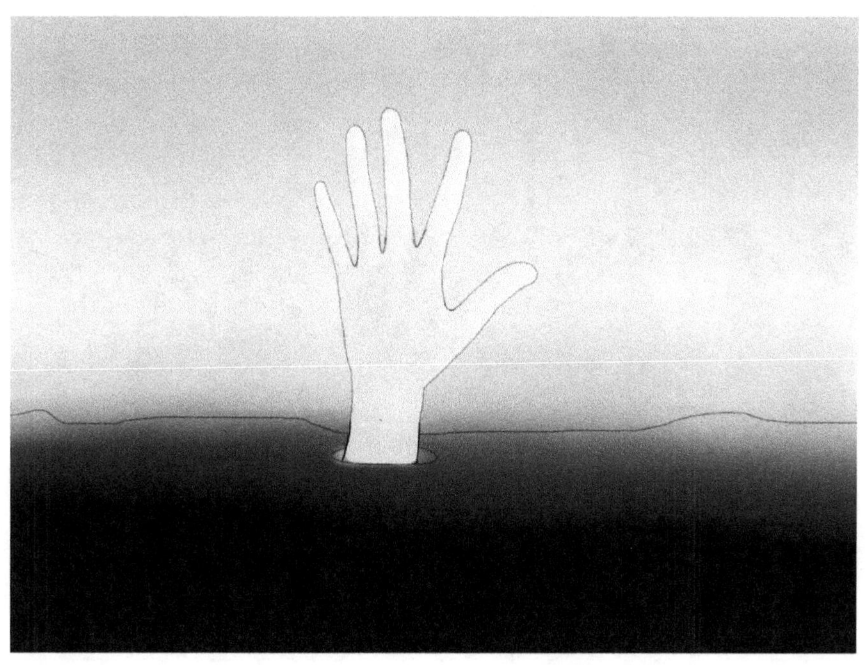

He called out to his parents to save him. He did not have the energy to swim to shore.

His father jumped into a small boat and rowed out, saved his son, and brought him to shore.

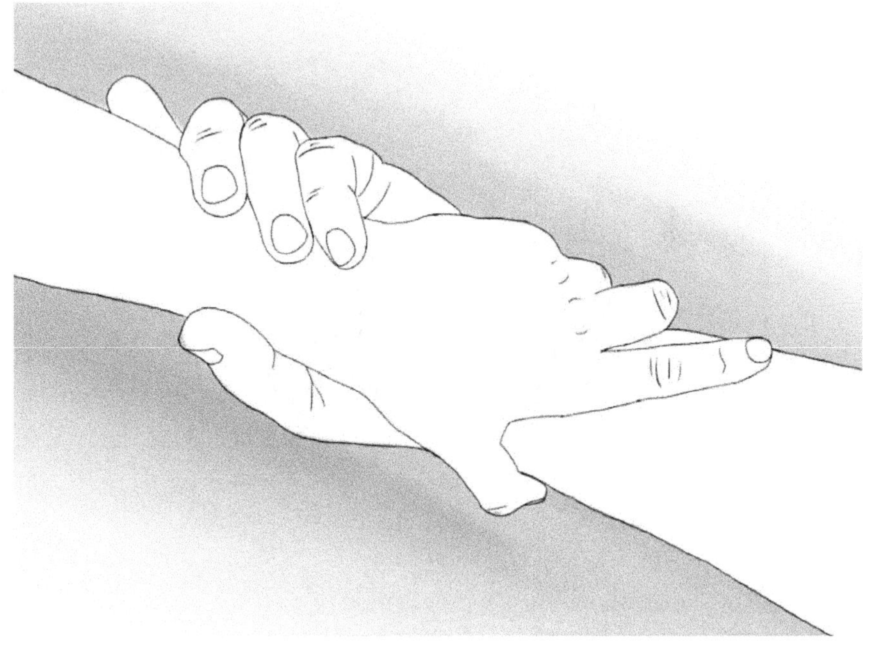

His mother cleaned him up and fed him and the boy regained his strength.

Amazingly, and to the shock of his parents, he swam back to the middle of the lake.

For weeks on end, the parents would stay by the lake and rescue their son again and again.

They feared for his life and hoped he would realize that if this continued he would die soon.

Their lives were also falling apart because of their son's actions. His parents argued about what to do.

ENDING NUMBER ONE

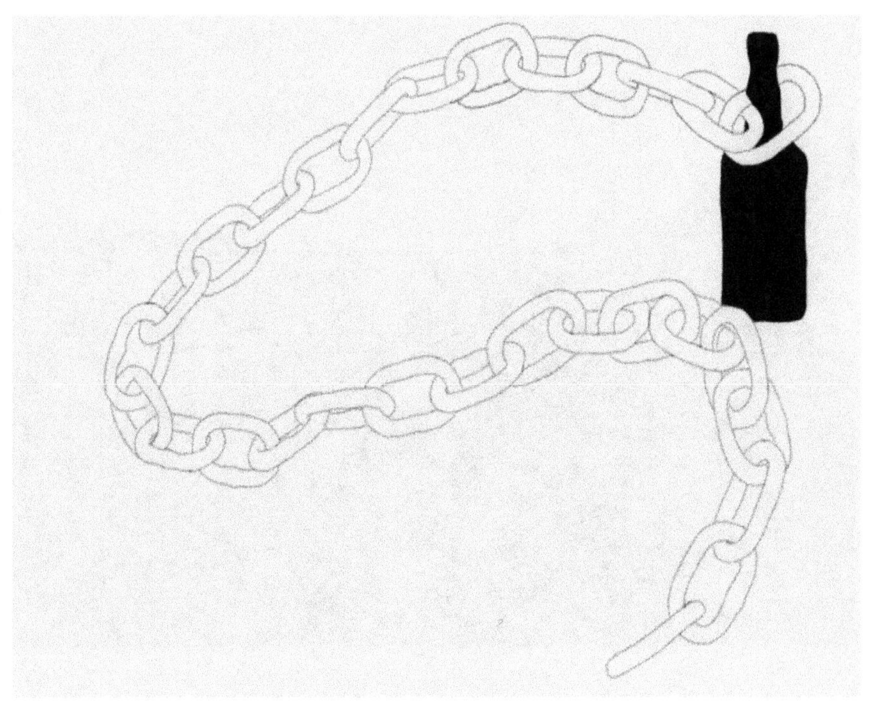

The parents loved their son and stayed by the lake day by day.

When he would panic and began to drown, they saved him.

However, as soon as he regained his strength he was back in the lake.

They noticed over time that the young man was growing weaker and weaker.

Finally, one evening the son began to sink again. The father went out to save him but he was gone.

The parents were devastated. They always questioned whether they could have handled the situation better.

ENDING NUMBER TWO

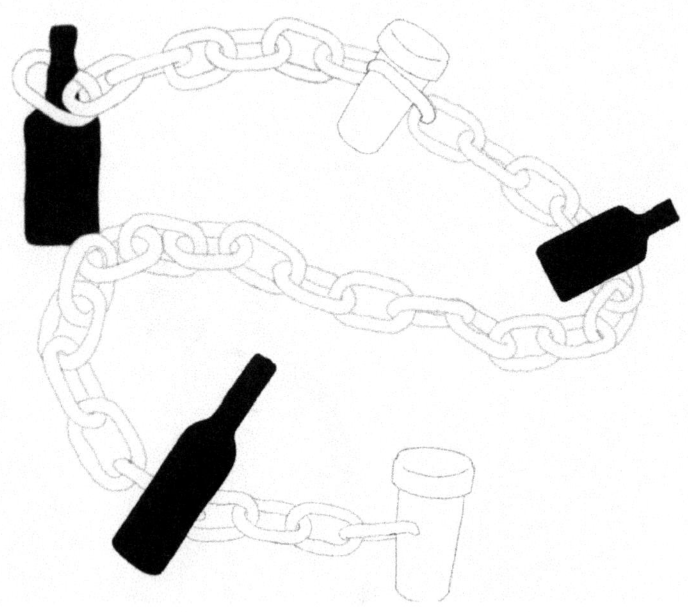

The parents loved their son and stayed by the lake day by day.

When he would panic and began to drown, they saved him. However, as soon as he regained his strength he was back in the lake.

They noticed over time that the young man was growing weaker and weaker.

They never gave up and devoted every moment to saving their son.

The farm failed and their lives were ruined.

They lost touch with family and the community.

On their deathbed they wondered, who is going to save our son now?

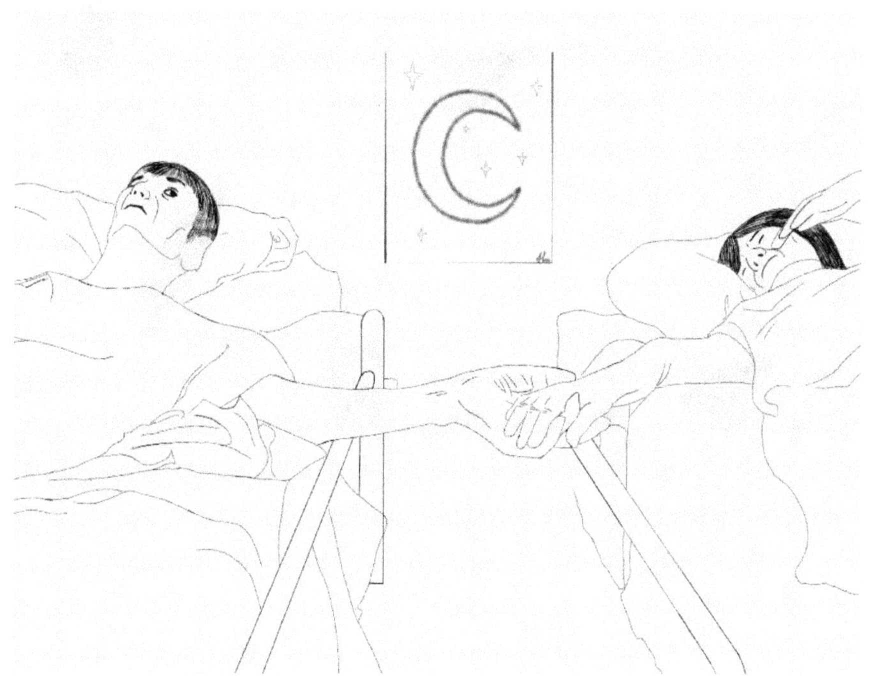

ENDING NUMBER THREE

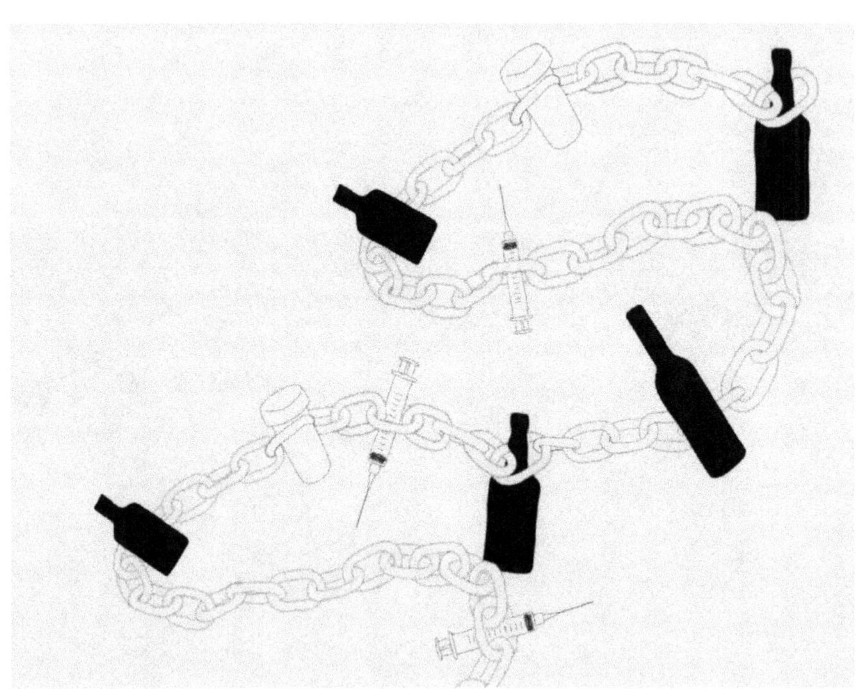

The parents felt they were enabling their son's ability to keep going back to the lake and decided to not go to the lake anymore.

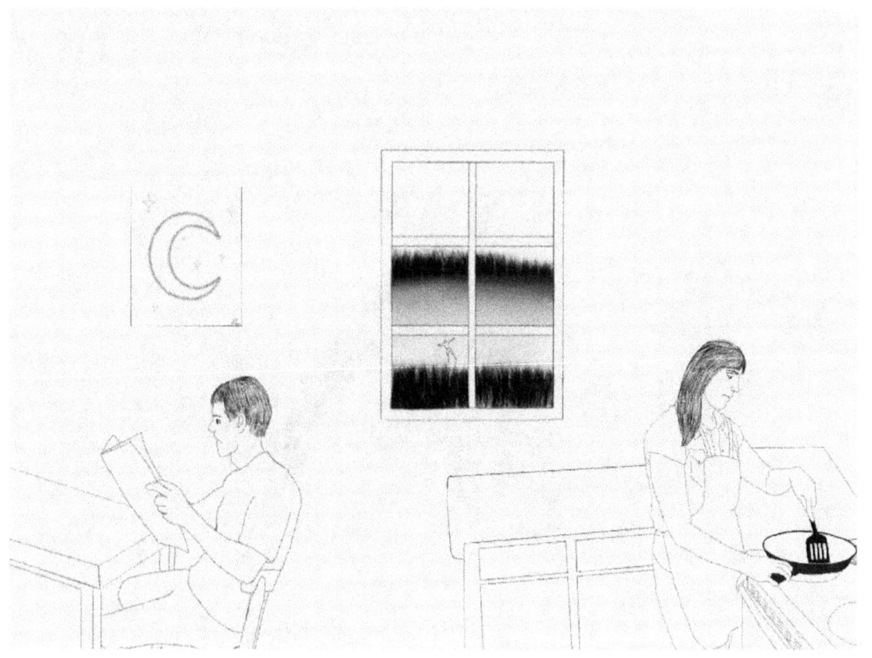

They knew it was a risk, but the only way he would stay out of the lake was to swim out and decide to stay out for good.

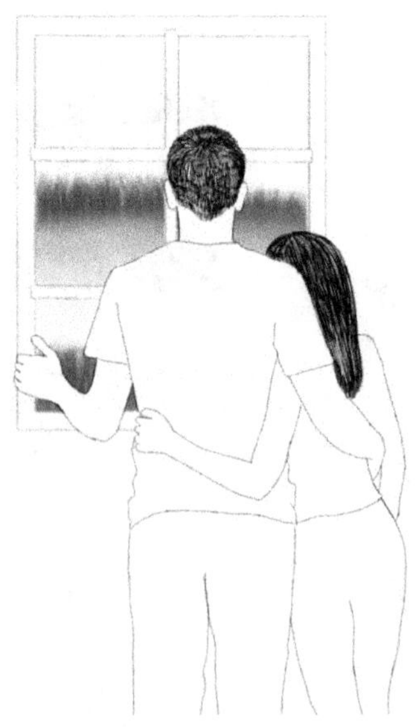

They were worried sick.

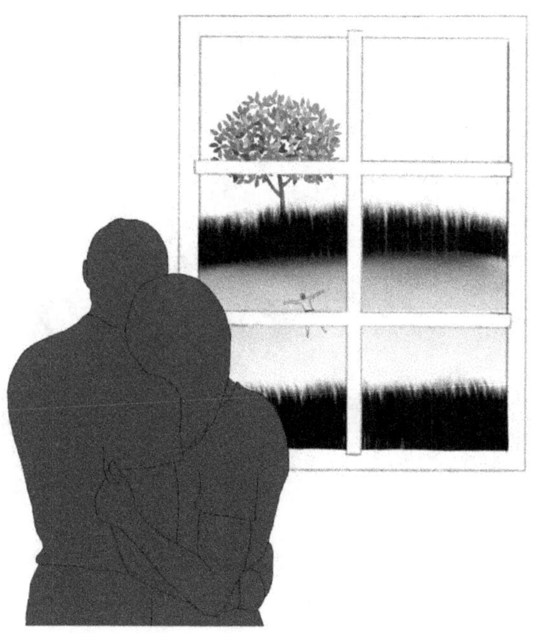

Then, their son walked in the house asked his parents for real help and he got better.

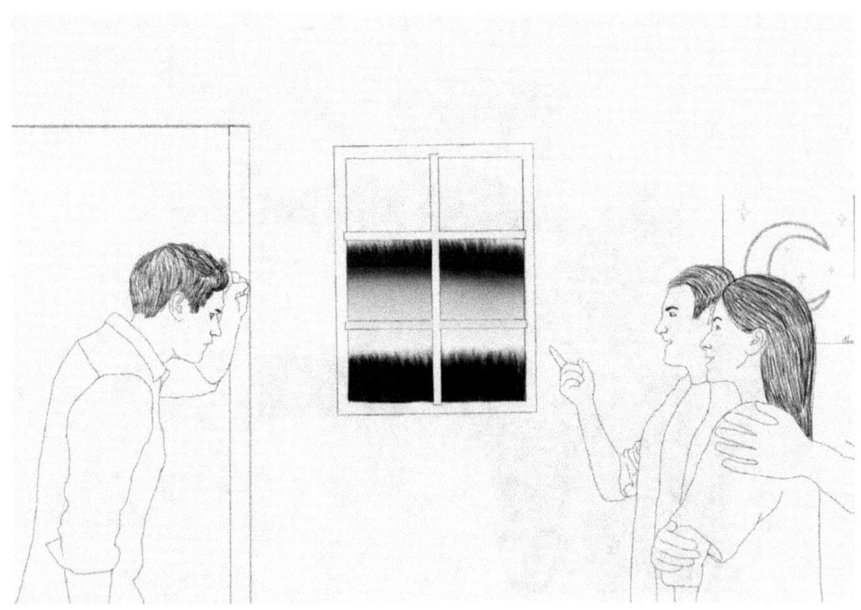

The son received professional help and joined a support group.

A few months later, father and son drained the lake and all was well again.

ENDING NUMBER FOUR

The parents felt they were enabling their son's ability to keep going back to the lake and decided to not go to the lake anymore.

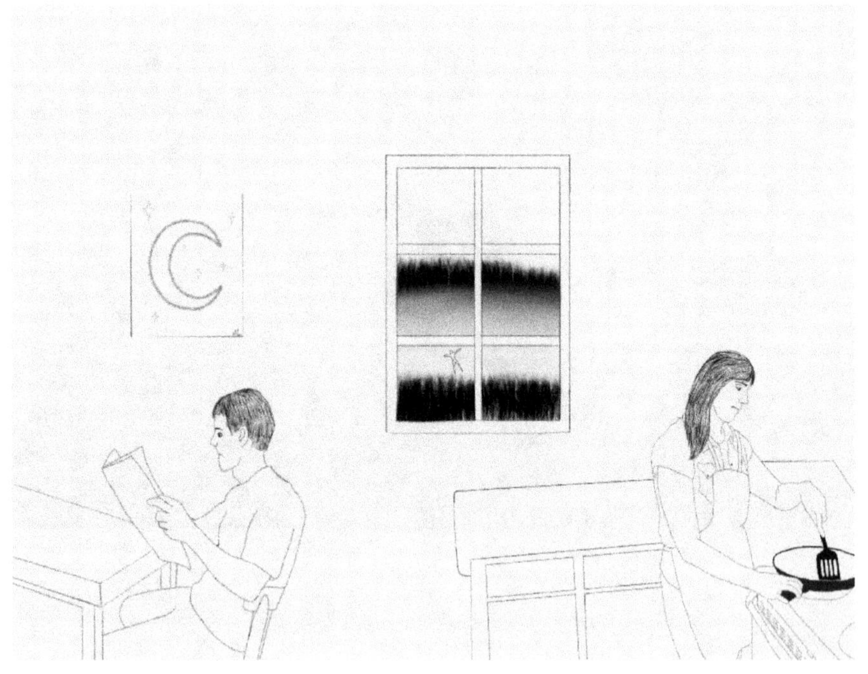

They knew it was a risk, but the only way he would stay out of the lake was to swim out on his own and decide to stay out.

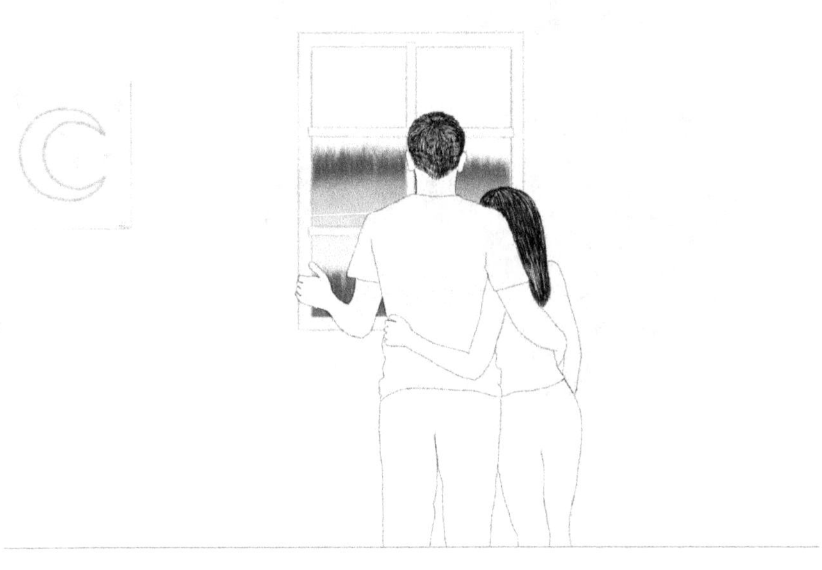

They were worried sick.

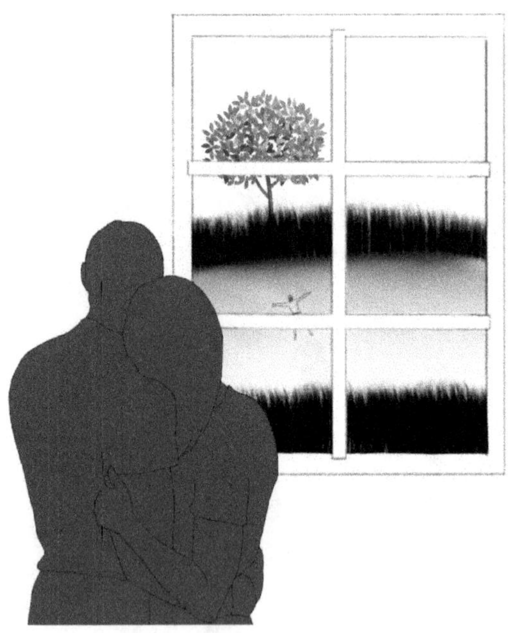

After a while, they got word that their son had drowned in the lake.

They always questioned whether they could have handled the situation better.

<u>To The Family</u> - There is no one right answer and it is not your fault.

Why Doesn't My Addict Just Quit?

Addiction is a disease!

Many parents, spouses and loved ones, just like the parents of the boy who could not stay out of the lake, are absolutely baffled by the addict's inability to quit. The addict loses their job, goes to jail, loses their marriage, has their children taken away, becomes homeless and they unbelievably continue to drink, drug, or both. In some cases, the family watches the addict stop for a period of time and begin to turn their life around. There is great relief for all involved. They take a sigh of relief and make the fateful mistake of letting their guard down. Our parents of the piano prodigy make this mistake again and again.

They see the benefits of the addict not using and then are shocked to see them start again and lose everything. Well, if you don't understand why your loved one does this, then you are fortunate. You do not have the disease of addiction. You will never experience the pain, misery, hopelessness, and confusion of the addict. But, this does not shield you from the pain of watching and experiencing this occurring to a loved one time and again. However, if you thoroughly understand the disease of addiction, then maybe you will be better armed to deal with, and help, the addict in your life. Even if you can't directly experience the disease you can learn about the disease and what it does to the addict.

Yes, I said disease! The National Institute on Drug Abuse defines addiction as a chronic, relapsing disorder characterized by compulsive drug seeking and use despite adverse consequences. It is considered a brain disorder, because it involves functional changes to brain circuits involved in reward, stress, and self-control, and those changes may last a long time after a person has stopped taking drugs. Do not believe the ignorant and uninformed that addiction is a lack of self-control. Do not be fooled by the notion that once the addictive substance is out of the addict's system that recovery has occurred.

I will give insight into the disease of addiction through my experience as an alcoholic. The disease is the same for any drug. Remember, alcohol is a drug just like any other. When I was young, if you asked me what I wanted to be when I grew up, I would never have said an alcoholic. I dreamt of playing professional football or being a marine biologist. I certainly would not have described the dream of being hopelessly addicted to alcohol. I would not have said I wanted alcohol to be the most important thing in my life. I never would have said I wanted to be totally controlled and enslaved by alcohol. Despite my desires, that is exactly what I grew up to be. I didn't have a horribly dysfunctional childhood. I was a normal well-adjusted child with loving and supportive parents; a stable family life; and a lot of friends.

The disease manifested itself in me in two ways; physically and mentally. When I took that first drink, I craved more. Once the drink was inside me, I would not stop until I ran out, exhausted all means to get more, or just passed out. I would often, knowing better, go out late at night and drive drunk to feed my physical craving. When I reawakened, or truthfully, came too, the first thing I thought of was how to get the next drink.

A person free of this ailment may occasionally party too much one night. However, when they wake the next morning with a hangover, the furthest thing from their mind is to have more. They will generally shy away from drinking for a while. In fact, those mornings generally started for me with the thought *why the hell did I do that. I will never do that again.* However, eventually that feeling to abstain was immediately replaced with the overwhelming desire to have a drink.

I found very early in my teenage years that I could drink more than my peers drank and I skillfully maintained myself, proud of the fact that I could drink anyone under the table. I could hold my liquor and rarely got sick and threw up. I had no clue that this was a potential warning sign of alcoholism. The more I drank the more it took to get the effect I desired. So naturally, to get that feeling from a week before or a month before, I drank more until I got the effect I desired.

Eventually, I became physically addicted to alcohol. In the end, I couldn't go more than two and a half hours without taking a drink. If I went any longer, I would begin to shake and feel sick. This is the beginning stages of Delirium Tremens (DTs). The DTs are a death sentence to an alcoholic if not treated immediately and often in a medical setting. The body goes into shock and the organs shut down resulting in death. So, to prevent the onset of the DTs I ensured I had alcohol in my system 24/7. The only way an alcoholic this advanced can avoid the DT's is to continue to stay intoxicated. In other words, the alcoholic is using the poison that is killing them as medicine to keep from dying.

Does this sound insane? It absolutely is, and that is one reason why addiction is a brain disorder. Although the constant intoxication wards off the DT's, the long-term damage to the liver, kidneys, heart, pancreas, and brain, will kill the alcoholic unless a tragic accident takes the alcoholic first. This physical addiction to alcohol did not manifest itself immediately; it was a slow and steady progression into full-blown physical addiction. For certain classes of drugs, especially heroin, cocaine, and methamphetamine, this full-blown addiction manifests itself much quicker.

Let's look at my experience. More times than I can remember, during my slide into active addiction to alcohol, I said I must either stop or moderate my drinking. I would make promises to myself that I had to do something. I knew deep down I was on a path to disaster.

First, I would try to moderate. I tried switching from whiskey to beer or wine. I attempted to have less in the house by buying smaller bottles, only to run out and drive intoxicated to get more. I tried to cut down slowly in an attempt to drink myself sober. I would try to limit my intake when I had to attend an important event. However, once I took that first drink, all plans to moderate went away like the drinks I devoured. There was no stopping the insatiable desire to drink more. That is the physical craving.

Then I tried to stop altogether and quit cold turkey. I thought, if I do not drink the first one, I will not start the cycle. This is where the most insidious part of the disease kicks in, the mental obsession. I found, despite the fact that I did not have alcohol in my system, I could not stop thinking about taking a drink. The thought of a drink grew more intense the longer I stayed away from it. I tried to use all the willpower I could muster not to take that first drink. Then the mental obsession overrides any willpower I have and I end up taking that first drink. As the hours pass, the desire to take a drink grows ever stronger until the point that I cannot think of anything else.

Finally, I surrender to the overwhelming desire and take that first drink and all is lost again. This starts the physical craving and the cycle starts again. Once the total physical addiction sets in, it is a triple whammy; mental obsession, physical craving, and physical addiction. It is classic irony. When I tried to control my drinking, I could not enjoy it and when I tried to enjoy my drinking, I couldn't control it.

Then comes the countless and worsening bottoms. In my first book, "A Drunks Tale from a Living Hell to Freedom", I described the mental distress of my personal bottom. Here is how I described it:

"I have stood at the gates of a personal hell, lost in a downward spiral. I looked up from the abyss at what was seemingly an insurmountable climb to a place that I was not sure existed. I was gazing at a strange world with normal, happy, well-adjusted people, a foreign world in which I did not fit. I was a drunk, an alcoholic who drank to live and lived to drink. Drinking was my only means to function, and drinking was the only way not to get sick. Drinking was killing me, and yet every ounce of my being told me I had to drink. I was alone in my disease and thought no one understood what I was going through. I surrounded myself with other drunks like me. It was in this world that I was dying, wrapped in a chemical sense of comfort. These fellow drunks did not judge me. They liked who I was, even though I hated who I was. I needed them, and they needed me. Still, I was miserable, embarrassed, and scared. I did not realize until much later that they were lost too. Cloaking myself in a mask of normalcy, I hid my suffering and eased the pain with more alcohol. With all of that spinning around my brain in a tornado of confusion, I did the only thing I knew how to do. I did the only thing I thought made me feel normal and content: I drank."

This is why even lengthy stays in rehabilitation centers alone rarely work. You may ask, why do they have such a low success rate? They are in a controlled environment filled with medical personnel and trained professionals. Although a critical and lifesaving first step, it is just the first step to recovery. The detox process and the education in the rehabilitation centers only gets the substance removed from the addict's system and launches the preliminary process of developing coping techniques to deal with the mental obsession. But that is rarely and almost never enough to recover. The mental obsession can last years and in most cases, the rest of the addict's life after release from inpatient treatment. The temptation and access to obtain and use addictive substances is mostly absent in the rehabilitation centers.

However, once released, all the access to and the

temptation is present. That is why the rehabilitation centers preach a strict regimen of aftercare. The addict must continue a daily regimen of treatment for the remainder of their lives.

In other words, after the onset of the addiction, it must be treated as what it actually is; an incurable but treatable disease. For example, if a person had diabetes, they have an incurable disease. However it is treatable through insulin, diet, and exercise. If the diabetic strictly follows the treatment regimen, they will live a long and happy life. If the diabetic stops treatment, the diabetic will get ill and die years before their time.

There is no difference with the disease of addiction. The addiction is treatable through the lifelong treatment for the mental obsession or disorder and total abstinence. **The lifelong treatment for the mental obsession sets the addict up for lasting success by remaining unwaveringly abstinent from their drug of choice and all mind altering substances to include legal forms like alcohol.**

Lifesaving treatment is available through counseling, Alcoholics Anonymous, Narcotics Anonymous, and other programs. A lifetime of aftercare is the only proven successful prevention for relapse.

Why is it so hard for the sick addict to ask for help? I was no exception. I repulsed at the notion to ask for help. Again, my story may give some insight. I suffered for years with this disease; the last ten years were the worst as I continued to spiral out of control. I knew I had a problem that was destroying my life. The sicker I got the more I realized that I could not solve this problem on my own and that baffled me.

I was relatively successful for most of my life. In high school I got good grades with little effort. I played High school football and division three college football. As an officer in the Army I led Platoons, Companies, and a Battalion. As a Department of the Army civilian supervisor I led teams of over thirty professionals. I solved their problems and counseled them to succeed. If I could lead so many over the years, I thought I could easily solve this problem. But despite my talents and skill, this disease had me beaten. No matter how hard I tried to control, moderate or quit altogether, the mental obsession overwhelmed me.

Fear and embarrassment also prevented me from asking for help. The fear was that I had relied on alcohol for so long; I did not know how to live without the drink. It was my go-to medicine for every situation and although it was not working anymore, it was all I knew. The embarrassment was I did not want anyone to know my secret. This included my wife, children, co-workers, and supervisors.

I don't know for sure why I finally asked for help. Many of my fellow alcoholics and addicts call it a "brief moment of clarity". I knew I was days, weeks, and maximum months from bringing my already crumbling life down on top of me and it was do something or die. I realized that the medicine (alcohol) that I was taking to keep from getting sick was the same poison that was killing me**. Let me state that again, the medicine I was taking to not get sick was the poison that was killing me in the first place!!**

I was in a bathroom stall at work sneaking a drink to stop the shaking and survive until lunch. When I exited the stall and looked at myself in the mirror, I was disgusted at what a saw in the mirror. I said to myself, *you are such a piece of shit, how could you let this get so far*. That was my moment of clarity.

Knowing what I had to do but still frightened, I went

back to my desk and called the employee assistance office and asked, "If I tell my boss I am an alcoholic and need help, can I get fired?" The voice on the other end, who I now have a professional relationship with, simply stated, "They are bound by law to help you with no retributions." So, I took a deep breath and walked into the Colonel's office, sat down and said, "This is the most personally and professionally embarrassing thing I have ever said. I am an alcoholic and I need help." This was my start to my long journey to sobriety. I simply had to be honest with myself and that was the hardest thing I have ever done.

This is what your addict is going through. They may appear tough, strong, and independent on the outside. They may claim they got the situation under control. However, like me, they are scared, isolated, confused, and in a personal hell. If they come to you and ask for help, that is a great first step. However, it is the first step of a long but lifesaving journey. Remember the only happy ending in Boy in the Middle of the Lake story was the one where the boy asked for help.

My years of continuous sobriety started with me being honest with myself and others on that fateful day in the Colonel's office, followed by a stay in inpatient rehabilitation and followed up with outpatient rehabilitation. My continued success is a direct result of my commitment to a lifetime of after care. Today I am healthy, happy, and a productive member of society. However, if I stop treating my disease, I am guaranteed a destructive and deadly relapse.

Remember, the addict suffers from a brain disorder. When in active addiction (using), the brain disorder amplifies at an exponential rate. Many of us in recovery refer to this brain disorder as "out there in the madness". The addict in fear of withdrawals will prey upon the easiest targets. Unfortunately, that usually is the family because they are the easiest to manipulate. Understand that you are not alone when you feel the pain and confusion of the addict taking advantage of you. Your frustration and bewilderment is natural. Remember even the most naturally honest and trustworthy person when in the grips of addiction will become a chronic liar and a thief to feed the addiction.

The Destruction of the Family

Do not allow the addict to drag the family down also.

There is no doubt that the addict has a devastating impact on the family, close friends, employers, and coworkers and frankly, everyone they come in contact with. Our boy who just could not stay out of the lake inflicted a lifelong barrage of emotional and financial devastation on his parents. Every addict in successful recovery, I work with and attend treatment with, did not realize fully the emotional pain, financial burden, and misery they caused the ones that loved them until they were participating in a life-time program of recovery. Even the most blatant examples of direct assault on the family such as stealing items from the home and pawning them, stealing credit cards, jewelry, and cash is partially lost to the addict while they are in this maddened state.

The addict is in a desperate state of mind. The fear of the pain and suffering of withdrawal overrides any logical or moral thought. They will state with full belief when questioned about their addiction, "I am not hurting anyone but myself" and believe that statement. The addict will lie to the point they believe their own lies. They are ashamed to admit to themselves or others they need help. The addict lives in fear of living their life without the drink or drug. Yes, the addict is very sick and should be treated as a sick person. This does not mean they are not responsible for their actions. They still are accountable for what they do to hurt others.

Financial loss due to the addict's behavior is destructive to the family, but it pales in comparison with the emotional stress and devastation of the addict's unwitting assaults on the family. **The family gets sick right along with the addict.**

The family begins to experience strong feelings of fear, depression, frustration, anger, heartbreak and resentment. The deep desire to save the addict is constantly crushed by the countless unsuccessful but well intentioned attempts to help the addict. Family members will fight and argue to the point of entire families falling apart due to the stress caused by the addict. Some family members are willing to destroy their own lives and the family to save the addict as demonstrated by the parents of the Boy in the Middle of the Lake and the father of our piano prodigy. Still others will take the opposite extreme and develop a hatred and resentment toward the addicted family member like the mother of the piano prodigy. **Do not hate the addict, if you have to hate something, hate the disease!**

In many cases the family suffers far worse than the addict. The family must guard against being sucked down with the addict. You cannot help the person you love if you are sick also. Anger, resentment, fear, detachment, stress, and depression are forms of sickness the family can experience as a side effect of the addict. Rarely can a sick person effectively help another sick person.

The family must understand that the addict must not

only want to recover but must be willing to take definitive action to recover. The family must realize that the mental disorder may cause the addict to say or do the right things for the moment to gain some trust in the true attempt to continue the addictive behavior. When the addict lies and steals in this manipulative fashion, they inflict the greatest financial and emotional pain on those that love them. This behavior is driven by all components of the disease, the uncontrollable craving, mental obsession, and fear of withdrawal. These feelings are overwhelming to the addict and cannot ever be underestimated.

Why does the addict have such an impact on the family and why does it persist for years? The answer is love, blind hope, and denial. First there is love. We love the person and do not want to believe that they are inflicting such pain on the family. The love drives us to protect them in any way imaginable. Parents especially feel a responsibility to do anything to help their child.

Second, there is blind hope. We hope that somehow, someway, they will come to their senses and just quit using and all will be well. We are hoping and praying for a miracle that rarely comes from hope alone.

Finally, there is fear and denial. The family is in fear which leads to denial. We just do not want to believe that the person, we care for so deeply, has changed in such a negative and destructive way. This finally leads to the family getting sick right along with the addict. It manifests itself in anger, depression and a feeling of helplessness. The reaction will differ for each family member. Some will lash out in anger and drive the addict further away. Some family members will shift from impulsive outbursts to heroic and fruitless attempts to play the hero. All this stems from a lack of knowledge and denial.

Acceptance is the key! The family's total acceptance that they are dealing with a person who has a disease is the first step. Accepting that you cannot will or force the person to change is a simple but brutal truth. This is difficult especially for parents who feel they can have a direct impact on their child. They feel in their hearts that years of teaching the child good sense, right from wrong, and morals will win the day. This is an example of underestimating this powerful disease.

Equally critical is the realization that you cannot control the addict but you can control how you deal with the addict. This is the beginning of a united and healthy family that has a chance to help the addict. The family can now develop a plan of action and be totally united when dealing with the active addict. They must stand together and decide how and to what extent they help the addict. They must focus on one goal, which is long-term recovery for the sick addict. The family may require counseling themselves too, especially if they have already been deeply affected by the situation. Prominent support groups include AL-Anon and Alateen have proven extremely effective for families. **Never forget, the family cannot truly help the addict if they are sick themselves!**

Dr. Jekyll or Mr. Hyde

Your loved one is already a slave to the addiction. Do not become a slave to the addict.

Dr. Jekyll and Mr. Hyde, a classic novella published in 1886 by Scottish author Robert Louis Stevenson and adapted in the many stage plays and classic horror movies, has spawned the now common phrase "Jekyll and Hyde". The term has been used to describe persons that display two distinct sides emotionally.

In this case I use the term to refer to the addict as two distinct persons in one. The core person is usually a very good person and the person you love (Dr. Jekyll). The other, the addict (Mr. Hyde), is capable of horrifyingly insane anti-social behavior. It is often difficult to tell these two apart because they are in the same body. The extremely cunning and manipulative nature of Mr. Hyde will enable him to hide behind the mask of Dr. Jekyll, appearing honest and forthright fooling all around them.

This is exactly what we experience with the addict. Below is the core question we must ask ourselves. **I am cur-**

rently helping my loved one (Dr. Jekyll) or am I being manipulated by the addict (Mr. Hyde) to destroy and ultimately kill my loved one? This is the trap and the biggest mistake the family will make. They, in a loving attempt to help the one they love, will actually be helping the addict kill the person we are trying to save.

Here, I ask you to change your perception of that person you love so dearly. This will be difficult and the whole family must come to terms with the following fact. You must accept that there are two people taking up residence in that one body. One person is the wonderful person that is slipping away from the family and the other person is ready to destroy anyone who tries to get in his way. If you want the wonderful person back, you must not get fooled by the addict. The addict (Mr. Hyde) is a formidable foe to both the addicted person and the family. You must treat Mr. Hyde as the enemy. His sole mission is to kill the person you love.

Easier said than done! The enemy right now knows you better than you know him. The addict will come to you asking for help. They will make up any excuse to trick and manipulate you to fund their habit or bail them out of a jam. The request usually is financial. It could be something as simple as twenty or forty dollars for a car part. Always be wary of these requests. These small and even dollar amounts are just what the addict needs to get their next temporary fix and avoid withdrawals. It is amazing how many times the addict in my life has car trouble.

The addict will do anything and everything in their power to make you feel guilty for refusing what appears to be a small request you can easily afford. The pressure can become relentless and all consuming. I admit, it has gotten so bad that I actually gave the money, knowing it is probably a lie, to just stop the begging and get some peace. That is me getting sick right along with the addict.

Do not make the mistake I made in the past. I was just aiding and abetting the addict (Mr. Hyde) and his quest to destroy the person (Dr. Jekyll). Now, if the request comes, I will say something like this: "OK, get in my car and we will go the auto parts store and buy the part and I will help you put it in." This will, in most cases, result in a barrage of anger and accusations of lack of trust. This is just another attempt of manipulation and guilt by the addict, Mr. Hyde. The truth was there is no problem with the car.

What if there is a small child or children involved? Many addicts have children. It boggles the mind of someone who has never been addicted to drugs and alcohol that the addict will not get, and stay, clean for their children. Yes, they will put their children in danger through neglect while they are seeking and using their drug of choice. Again, we must accept the fact that the disease is stronger than any bond of love.

Is there any doubt that this is a mental disorder? Any state of mind that would allow the strong biological bond between parent and child to be ignored and destroyed, can only be described as a mental defect. Remember, I said I was a slave to alcohol. All addicts are slaves to their drug also. They are under the complete control of their alter ego Mr. Hyde.

Here is the trap the addict will set for you. A good person would never let the innocent suffer and the addict knows that. The addict will use the care of the children, most likely your grandchildren, as a way to secure money for their drug of choice.

For the parents of very young children, money for doctor appointments, diapers, and food are just some examples the addict will use to get money from the family. They often divert some, or all, of the money to their drug of choice. How can anyone say no to such a request?

As with the car part, it is better to purchase those items or ask for the doctor bill and pay it yourself. You may find that no bill actually exists. Even if you follow this technique, the addict will adjust right along with you by shifting funds to drugs and alcohol and burdening you with the financial responsibility of caring for the raising of their children.

The addict will adjust to what you are willing to give and make it work to their advantage. Does this sound like a war? Well it is! You must become as flexible and cunning as the addict. Yes, this is war. The war is not against the person you love but against the addict that possesses their body. You must make that distinction. When children are involved, you may have to get social services involved if you feel the children are being neglected or abused. Lack of action could end in the worst possible disaster, the death of a small child.

How do you know which person you are dealing with? This is tricky and I can only suggest these techniques based on my previous experience, previous failures, stupid mistakes, and the experience of the people I work with and those who work with me in recovery. We have to determine definitive signs where all involved feels they are dealing with a person in solid recovery not the addict. All involved means the entire family that is affected by the addict. You must be consistent as a family. Even normal non-addicted children will play mom against dad to get what they want, so you have to guard against this advanced form of manipulation.

Having no drugs or alcohol in your system is not clean nor sober! Despite the fact that the person does not have drugs in their system at the moment, the addict is still sick. Alcoholics call this being a "Dry Drunk". A dry drunk is abstaining from alcohol but still having the overwhelming desire to drink.

A dry drunk is a ticking time bomb. The addict and alcoholic are depriving themselves of a substance they crave deeply. This creates a massive void. If there is nothing to fill the void previously filled by drugs and alcohol, the addict becomes miserable and is doomed to relapse. Remember, the mental obsession still lives within.

Many families and the addicts themselves universally misunderstand this fact. The addict needs to be completely detoxified and working a serious recovery program to treat the mental disorder to be considered remotely clean and sober. Even at this point, the term "trust but verify", is a watchword that will pay dividends. Do not let the addict make you feel guilty when you verify everything before giving them assistance. Remember, Mr. Hyde is always there, the addict is never cured. Recovery is a lifelong process.

Over time, recovery will happen and the addict will return to the normal well-adjusted person you knew and are glad to have back in your life. Despite that fact, trust and privilege must be earned back slowly. It does not matter if they understand that, it is important that you understand it and stick to your guns. It is dangerous to return all the things and financial comfort quickly when an addict is in early recovery. The addict may feel they still have that former safety net they so cunningly took advantage of over the years and may take the chance walking that dangerous high wire of drinking and using again.

If you determine that your loved one is working an honest and thorough program of recovery, you can now begin to trust that you are actually communicating on an honest level again. You can clearly explain why you may not be ready to fully trust and provide 100% assistance yet. You can set the goals to the when, and how, you will assist again. Your assets are yours and you must remain in control. It is important to establish that open and brutally honest communication when the addict is sober enough to receive it.

Change Tough Love to Constructive Love

Earlier in this book, I described the self-prescribed preachers telling you what to do using these statements: "Use tough love. Cut them off." As we saw with the stories The Boy in the Middle of the Lake and with our piano prodigy, it is not that simple. I want us to throw these terms out the window!

Do this exercise:

Write them down on a piece of paper.

Use tough
love
Cut
them off

Then cross those terms out.

~~Use tough love~~

~~Cut them off~~

Finally, throw them in the trash or burn them. Let them fade away.

These ugly terms are gone forever.

We will now only display constructive love. Constructive love is a healthy type of love that gives the person a hand up not a handout. It is a positive form of enabling. It is assistance that helps the receiver without hurting the giver. It is an equal loving partnership between the giver and receiver. We will only positively enable Dr. Jekyll, the true person, through constructive love and never enable Mr. Hyde, the addict again.

Saying no, is a component of constructive love. Saying no to the addict is an attempt to save their life and preserve the family, and you should never feel guilty or allow the addict to make you feel guilty for a no. Giving the person you love the opportunity to recover on a daily basis is constructive love.

Let us start from the beginning. Remember our child piano prodigy that became addicted in college? The parents rushed to her aid and placed her in the best rehabilitation center possible. Luxury rehabilitation with beautiful rolling hills, private rooms, and therapeutic massage may not have been the way to go. Maybe a less expensive facility with fellow addicts in even more desperate circumstances would have made a better impact.

When she was released from the rehabilitation center, maybe instead of fulfilling her wishes to go right back to school, they could have made her stay home, continue treatment and get a job to pay for at least part of the future tuition. In our illustrated story, Boy in the Middle of the Lake, two endings saw the parents continue to stand vigil by the lake to protect him from drowning. Both of those endings ended in disaster. The parents took on 100% of the burden and consequences for their son's behavior and choices. They provided him a safety net to continue to feed the addiction.

For our piano prodigy, throwing a person right back in the environment that got them addicted is dangerous and simply put, never works. It is possible that despite her immense talent, that a music career and all the trappings that go along with that life may have been too much for the addict. Yes, it is a horrible thought to waste such talent, but it is certainly better than death! However, there is a possibility that after sufficient recovery that she could return to music. However, this is only possible when armed with the life tools obtained through long-term recovery.

Let us give the parents a break, call it I learning experience, and move on to the second event of crashing the car, DUI, and being thrown out of school. The parents reacted and followed the same recipe that did not work before. They hired a lawyer to reduce the DUI charges, paid to send her back to the rehab, bought her a replacement car, and got her into another college. Again, after a short period, she relapsed and the cycle of addiction and the cycle of enabling continued. Everyone was getting sicker at the same time. There is a saying, "if nothing changes, nothing changes." Neither the parents nor their daughter changed, and they were shocked the situation continued to worsen.

Constructive love would have been allowing their daughter to be accountable for her actions. Maybe if the daughter felt the full consequences for the DUI it may have made her more receptive to listen and learn in the rehabilitation center. If the parents forced the daughter to get a job to earn the money for a car, then maybe she would have worked harder to stay clean to reach that goal. If the parents made the agreement that they would help with tuition for another school, if she continued treatment after the stay in the rehabilitation center, then maybe she may have had more motivation to stay clean.

Recovery takes time, and the longer the addict works a program of recovery the stronger the recovery becomes. I remind you that you are not in control of the recovery. It is ultimately up to the addict. You are just providing constructive love.

Remember, our boy in the middle of the lake, three of the four endings resulted in the boy's death or the parents dying in heartbreak. In only one scenario the boy recovered, because the addict took the responsibility for his disease. We have to face the fact that even our best efforts may prove fruitless. However, constructive love gives the family a fighting chance.

Let us get back to our piano prodigy. What if the parents were properly educated on the disease of addiction? The parents are united with a plan that places the responsibility and burden on their daughter. They are willing to put forth assistance based on her willingness to work her recovery.

This way they forge a partnership in the recovery process for them and their daughter. They are not tearing their lives apart right along with their daughter. It may take years for their daughter to be ready to takes the steps to overcome the addiction. Remember, if the family is destroyed, along with the addict, then when the addict is ready, they will not be capable to help when it truly counts.

We also crossed out the term, "cut them off". Never should we just completely cut someone out of the family. The door should be left open for when the addict is ready to be honest with themselves and the family. The assistance provided should be commensurate with the level of the addict's commitment and the visible and consistent work to stay clean and sober. There should be no gifts or rewards not earned. Instead, assistance should be encouragement to dig themselves out of the hole with possible carefully placed loans (not gifts) or matching funds for necessary items at best. This is giving a hand up as opposed to a handout.

We are in charge of the how, when, and why you help the loved one. We call the shots! We must know when we are dealing with the manipulative addict that is killing our loved one and when we are dealing with the actual sick person.

Often times the manipulative addict tricks us and

skillfully attempts to call the shots. We must say no more! If the help is not directly linked to their efforts to stay clean and sober, then the help must be withheld no matter how bad it makes you feel or how guilty the addict will try to make you feel. This is why the entire family must understand the plan and not waiver.

This is a life and death errand for the addict and yes, the entire family.

What Are the Signs of Recovery?

Recovery from an addiction is a slow process. It takes hard work, focus, and commitment to transform from the addict to a recovered person ready to become a trusted and productive member of the family and society. The addict must accept that they suffer from an incurable but treatable disease of the mind and body. The addict is never cured of the malady; the physical addiction will always be there waiting to take control when the addict starts using again.

However, the addict can go through a period of recovery and be recovered from the mental obsession or malady that drives them to drink or drug. The recovered state will only last if the addict treats that mental obsession daily. Fellowships such as Alcoholics Anonymous, Narcotics Anonymous, and other programs and counseling help in the daily maintenance of the mental part of the disease. The question we must ask is when will we be able begin to trust our loved one again? How do we know the addict inside of our loved one is not manipulating us yet again?

Here are some signs that recovery has begun.

They change their people they hang out with and replace them with more positive and productive people. Continuing to associate with the people they used to when actively drinking or using is dangerous and a warning sign that recovery may not be a priority to the addict. If the addict continues to associate with friends that still are using, they will inevitably fall prey to the mental obsession and use again. They may be trying to capture the essence of the party without actually engaging in the substance abuse. This never works.

Associating with people who are not using and others in a positive recovery program keeps the recovering addict away from temptation. They see the positive benefits of a life free of addiction and have a better chance of success. They feel a sense of accountability to their peers in recovery and do not want to let them down. If their friends are positive influences to the journey to sobriety, then they are in the right crowd.

They avoid the places and hangouts that they frequented in addiction.

You see them going to lengths to avoid the old places that got them in trouble. Going to these places are a temptation and must be avoided at all costs. Places like bars and clubs are places the addict must not go. Hanging at a friend's house that still uses, even to do something as innocent as watching a movie, is a risk.

In addition, a career change or delay may be necessary. For example, if the addict is a tattoo artist and works late in the evening tattooing drunk or high patrons, it may be necessary to find a new line of work. The job of a bartender is an example that does not require explanation. I have found people in recovery be able to handle such jobs and stay clean and sober, however, it is generally not possible until after years of recovery and even then, it can be a risk. Think of it this way, if you were highly allergic to bees, would you want a career as a beekeeper?

They avoid activities that fostered and encouraged drug or alcohol use.

Every person wants to and needs to have fun. Fun activities are important to a well-balanced life. A person in recovery must also find fun and pleasurable activities to balance their life.

However, we are creatures of habit and we only know about what we have experienced in the past. The addict must try new experiences that are void of alcohol and drug use being the center of the activity. Many recovery groups sponsor outings to parks with activities such as volleyball or softball. They coordinate trips to sober meetings and conferences. There are even sober cruises available.

What if the person in recovery loves a certain musical act or artist? The group is coming to town for possibly their farewell tour and the desire to see the act is deep and important. The recovering addict does not have to sit home and miss the show. They can go with another person, or persons, in recovery or a family member to ensure they do not slip due to temptation. They do not have to miss family functions such as weddings and birthday parties. They just bring a sober friend along.

They are generally excited about recovery.

A great signal is the person in recovery gets excited about the process. You can see it. The person is almost giddy about their transformation. They talk freely about the benefits of recovery and their development. They subscribe to social media sites that are recovery based. Recovery books begin to appear around the house. They talk about what they learned from others in recovery and brag about milestones people have reached. They credit their own personal successes to recovery and not themselves. This dramatic shift may shock you, but it is a great sign that change is happening.

They are consistent in attending treatment and do not have to be reminded to go.

Meetings and recovery activities become part of the daily routine as taking drugs or drinking was. They will pass on other activities if the activity conflicts with meetings or counseling. They may even get annoyed if they have to miss a recovery activity or session due to a work or family commitment.

They read recovery literature and seek out recovery videos, articles, and blogs on-line.

You will see them immersing themselves in everything they can find about recovery and the recovery community. They will in time compile an impressive library of recovery literature. They will start to travel to attend conferences with others in recovery. Using social media, they will participate in, and read, recovery blogs, Facebook pages, and Twitter pages focused on recovery. Key books you will see are the Big Book of Alcoholics Anonymous, Narcotics Anonymous, books on the twelve steps, and autobiographies from other successful recovering alcoholics and addicts.

They begin to look better and appear healthy.

The toll drug and alcohol abuse takes on the body and the addict's appearance is profound. You will see a person that is serious about recovery convert from the walking dead to a healthy and vibrant person.

They focus on hygiene and neatness.

If you ever walked into an apartment or house of a person in the madness of addiction, you would wonder, in most cases, why the place has not been condemned by the city. The addict generally can appear un-bathed and in some cases will wear the same dirty clothes for a day. Our person in recovery will begin to develop a new respect for themselves and their surroundings.

They become more responsible with money they earn.

The addict has often squandered countless amounts of money, to include the family's money. More than they could possibly account for. Many will do a turn-about and guard their newly earned money carefully. Sometimes they will swing so far the other way they will become cheap and miserly. This initial thrifty behavior is normal and the person will find a balance as their recovery progresses.

They may develop a sense of spirituality, which is encouraged in most twelve-step programs.

The twelve step programs highly encourage a relationship with the GOD of their understanding. The source of the spirituality may or may not come from a religious institution. It is a personal relationship with their concept of a higher power. It is a transformation from selfishness to selflessness. The programs suggest prayer and meditation as an integral part of beginning to live a spiritual life free of self-seeking and addiction.

They will become less selfish and attempt to be altruistic or selfless.

This person who seemed to only care about themselves and their drug or drink begins to transform into a more selfless and giving person. They will begin to help others and expect nothing in return. Their focus on giving away the gift of sobriety they were given is not only spiritual, it keeps them focused on their sobriety.

They will start showing the ability to control their emotions and deal better with anger, rage, fear, and sadness.

You will see a change in their ability to handle people and situations which in their addiction would throw them into a fit of anger, denial, or depression. They are learning coping skills to deal with life's day to day problems without turning to the crutch of drugs and alcohol.

They will become more resilient and demonstrate the ability to push through setbacks.

Resiliency is a skill all people need, whether addicted or not, to deal with life's twists and turns. Resilient people have the ability to withstand and adapt to stressful situations and adversity. You will find when they are faced with situations that used to cripple the addict, they begin to cope with them better.

They will begin to make amends.

They will begin to make amends to family, friends, employers, and everyone they hurt in addiction. They will pay back debts when possible or do other helpful things in an attempt to make up for their transgressions. They will be present when they were once absent. The most important amends is that they try every day to not repeat the mistakes of the past.

These are just general signs of recovery and they will vary from person to person. In short, they are regaining their grip on life and their place in society. Using these signs can give us a litmus test on when we can begin the process of trusting our loved one.

The recovering addict will want the trust to come quickly and may be disappointed that we are withholding that trust initially or slowly releasing the trust as they prove to us that they are taking the recovery process seriously. The proof we seek comes through actions, not promises.

Sometimes we may have to snatch back trust or a privilege when there is doubt of their total commitment. It is not our job to serve them. Our role is to be a positive enabler of recovery. We do not argue with our loved one, we simply state our expectations and what they need to display to gain our trust and access to our assets.

This should not be a secret plan. Our willingness to help and what it will take to gain your assistance should be clearly communicated, and if necessary, laid out in a contract. In fact, a written contract may be a technique worth exploring. This puts the burden on the addict and not on you. ***This is Constructive Love!***

This will sound insane. Do not get jealous of the recovery you have so longed for. How could I ever get jealous of such a positive outcome?

It happens more often than you think and here is why it occurs. The family often fights for years to save the addict. The family has been stymied and frustrated at every turn. They put up with lying, stealing, and all forms of deception. The addict does not just steal possessions, but steals time, energy, emotions, peace, and the sanity of everyone involved. The family sacrifices everything in the hope that they can get the person back they used to know.

Here is how it goes down. The addict finds a long-term solution that provides a freedom from addiction. The understanding that the solution requires daily treatment and action is now solidified in thought and action. They have rejected the people, places, and things from their addictive past. They associate with people with the winning solution. They do everything you hope for and you end up seeing them less than you did when they were out running the streets in active addiction.

This group of strangers has done more to help the person you lost in a short period than you could achieve after years of struggle. The reborn person spends all their free time working to ensure they never relapse again. They spend countless hours at meetings and clean and sober events and conferences. You know they are finally doing the right thing, but you feel abandoned and may feel like you failed in the past.

Do not worry or be jealous. It takes time for the person to find balance in their life. They must focus 100% of their time on fixing themselves. This may require them spending less time with you. They have to learn how to live all over again. If you have been their primary enabler, then they must learn to stand on their own. As recovery strengthens, they will learn how to balance recovery with family and the world. **Be patient and don't quit until the miracle happens.**

What are the Warning Signs for Relapse?

While we are looking for those positive signs that our loved one is recovering, we must also look for the signs that a relapse may be imminent or may have occurred. Even small changes can be a warning sign. Remember, our loved one is still very ill. They are suffering from a mental disorder and may not be as resilient as they try to appear.

Remember, it is difficult for anyone to admit they are struggling until it is generally a crisis. Even then, in crisis, they will find the easiest way to get through the moment and not be capable of seeing a long-term solution.

Here are some signs of relapse.

They begin to isolate themselves and withdraw from the family.

If you find the person in recovery beginning to isolate and withdraw from the family dynamic that is cause for worry. Becoming secretive or guarded may be a sign that they are slipping into activities that are not in keeping with the families stated expectations of the recovering person.

They begin to become too busy to go to meetings or counseling.

This may not be a direct sign that a relapse has happened but it is warning signal that the recovering person may be placing less stock in the recovery program and is beginning to think they can do this on their own. This is one of the biggest mistakes that will lead to a devastating relapse.

Often the person's life turns around so quickly and dramatically that they think they have the problem licked. They forget that they couldn't stay sober on their own and fall into the trap that they no longer need lifelong treatment. I have observed this happen to people with years of sobriety and sadly many of them die within months of the relapse.

They begin to reconnect with associates they knew in active addiction.

The recovering person made friends when they were actively drinking and using. They may feel a strong connection to those friends. If those friends are still actively drinking and using, they will be an irresistible temptation.

They feel the need to visit the bars or the parties where the primary focus is drinking or drug use.

We are not talking about restaurants that serve alcohol, although they should be avoided initially. A person in solid recovery will be able to frequent these places after a period of sobriety as long as the primary purpose is to go there for the food. We are talking about clubs, bars, and private parties where the main purpose is to drink or drug.

If this starts to occur, they may be missing some perceived excitement and fun of the past. They may be romanticizing about the early good times and forgetting the dark times. They may not even intend to pick up a drink or drug however, being in that environment is extremely dangerous.

Other priorities replace the excitement for their program of recovery.

If recovery is successful, the person will probably get a full time job. They will get involved in hobbies or interests. A romantic relationship may blossom or reignite. There may be opportunities to travel and vacation. All these things are gifts of sobriety. The addict cannot forget they have all these opportunities because they are treating their disease on a daily basis. If they fail to treat the mental obsession, the chances of relapse increase.

They begin to act out and show less patience.

The resiliency and ability to control emotions is a key sign of recovery. The loss of these coping skills is either a sign of losing focus on their program of recovery or worse that a relapse has occurred.

They start having trouble meeting their financial obligations.

This is a red flag! If a stable financial situation falls apart with no logical explanation than that is a sign of relapse.

They begin to ask to borrow money with increased frequency.

As with failing to meet bills this is a definite warning signal. The family should be wary of lending or giving money. Here is where the addict can be extremely cunning. They will go to different family members in succession and each member will not know what the others have provided.

Elderly grandparents are especially vulnerable and should be protected from cons and theft.

Their routines change.

Habits can be good or bad. A person in recovery normally develops positive habits or routines that aid in recovery. As they begin to alter their positive routines, they may be losing focus on recovery or possibly have relapsed.

They become secretive and become increasingly annoyed with inquiries about how they are doing.

The normally open person who freely talks about their recovery begins to speak less about recovery and gets annoyed or angered when the subject comes up in conversation.

Their physical appearance and hygiene begins to change.

Another red flag!

They show an inability to take care of simple things like household cleaning, and laundry.

Of course, you will know your loved one much better than anyone else will. A warning sign such as sloppiness may be a red flag for some but if your loved one was a slob before they became addicted, then that may just be them.

The key is to monitor the signs of recovery while painstakingly looking for those cracks in their delicate armor that are warning signs for relapse. When these signs emerge, being shy or worrying about your loved ones feelings should be the furthest thing from your mind. If you have been honest about your plan, and the conditions set by the family required to help, than these inquiries may annoy or upset the loved one but should not surprise them. **Remember, this is a life or death situation!**

A Deadly Pitfall

One deadly mistake I have seen addicts and family members make is the lack of understanding that once the person is addicted to any drug or alcohol that the addict must abstain from all other mind-altering substances. I once watched a member of my family offer a recovering heroin addict a glass of wine. I was shocked my family member did not know better, but this was my fault for not teaching the family the facts by ensuring they knew all aspects of the disease of addiction and what it takes to stay clean and sober.

Why was my family member wrong? The person was attempting to recover from an addiction to heroin. The person never displayed an issue with alcohol. So, the family member thought that an innocent drink was fine.

The person has relapsed twice on heroin since that event. I'm not saying that that drink caused the relapse; however, this is an example of lack of knowledge from family members.

The blame does not rest solely on the person who offered the drink, the blame rests mainly on the recovering heroin addict who was taught the fact that all mind-altering substances are dangerous. This is universally taught in rehabilitation centers and reinforced in AA and NA meetings. The addict in this instance chose to ignore the warning. Drug addicts will be faced with more innocent offers of alcohol and marijuana than they will ever face of their drug of choice and must guard against any mind altering substances entering the body.

Both drugs and alcohol affect the pleasure centers in the brain. Once addicted to a drug or alcohol the brain circuits have been altered and the addict is susceptible to either becoming addicted to the new substance or relapse on their drug of choice by lowering their inhibitions. They often begin to crave and seek the desired pleasurable effect that the original addictive drug gave them. **Yes, an alcoholic should not use drugs and a drug addict should not drink alcohol!**

The addict must never touch any brain altering substance if they want their recovery to last for their lifetime. This poses some issues with necessary prescribed prescription drugs for temporary or long term physical ailments. If the recovering addict has their wisdom teeth removed while in active recovery, the dentist will most likely prescribe an opioid based narcotic painkiller to ease in the recovery from the procedure. These drugs will also be prescribed for all types of surgeries and procedures.

The recovering addict, if working an honest program, will inform the dentist or doctor that they are in recovery and they will then prescribe a non-narcotic pain killer. Yes, less effective, but critical to prevent relapse.

I am an alcoholic and never had an issue with drugs. But, knowing these facts, I shy away from taking opioid based pain killers. I have had two surgeries while in recovery. One was to repair a hernia and the other was knee surgery. In both cases, I used non-narcotic pain relievers and managed fine.

I have heard many stories of people in years of successful recovery that accepted an opioid based prescription for a legitimate medical reason and taking the medication directly resulted to a relapse back to their original drug of choice. I have also witnessed people in solid recovery go through serious surgeries and successfully manage the pain through non-narcotic painkillers.

I realize there may be times that it is absolutely necessary to take these narcotic medications to manage pain resulting from an injury, surgery, or medical condition. If this is the case, it is highly suggested that the recovering addict request the lowest possible dose for the shortest duration to limit risk. The medicine should be held by a trusted family member and issued at the proper intervals and dose to the patient. The recovering addict should increase the frequency of meetings and involvement with the recovery community during, and immediately after, the regimen of medications is completed.

Developing a Plan of Action

If addiction affects the entire family, then recovery becomes a family affair.

We will now develop a plan based on constructive love. Constructive love is a partnership between the addict and the family. The family will do everything in its power to help the loved one (Dr Jekyll) recover, but will not fall prey to the addict (Mr. Hyde).

This love is solely focused on one goal, lasting recovery that returns the addict to becoming a healthy and productive member of society and the family. This love requires the family to trust but verify, and when in doubt hold back assistance. The family must not fall prey to emotional pleas. It requires the loved one to expect a level of scrutiny that may make them feel uncomfortable or untrusted.

Sounds tough and rigid but remember this is a life and death situation and must be treated that way. Not only does the addict need to control their emotions during this period of huge adjustment, the family must remain stoic and unemotional. This will ease argument and slowly show the loved one this is the new normal. Remember, all this is predicated on the love we have for this sick person.

Now that we know exactly what we are up against, and we are armed with the facts about the disease, we need to develop a plan that is focused on two critical goals. The first goal is to help the addict help himself or herself. The second goal is to ensure the family is not overwhelmed and ends up doing all the work. The entire family that the addict touches must be" all in". This may include very close friends of the family. Remember we are dealing with Dr. Jekyll, our loved one, and the formidable foe Mr. Hyde, the addict possessing him. Mr. Hyde will look for cracks in any family member's armor and exploit them.

The goal is singular and simple. We want our loved one to become truly clean and sober. This means the disease is placed in a state of remission and recovery blossoms.

First you must look at the entire family. How sick has the family become? How divided is the family on how to handle the addict? Understand that everyone is dealing with an untenable situation the best they can and with their best intentions. They most likely had no clue that they were dealing with someone with a disease. They were just not equipped to handle the situation.

It is time to forgive ourselves and each other and begin anew. Honest crosstalk and forgiveness between family members must occur before any plan of action is created. Professional counseling or the ALANON program may be necessary. Remember, sick people are ineffective when trying to help another sick person.

The addict is not just the elephant in the room; they are the elephant in the entire house and in the lives of the family and close friends. We must reduce this footprint to the addict being the elephant in one room. This room must be contained so the family can begin to live a normal healthy life again. Then they are poised to truly help the addict recover.

The plan should be extremely restrictive to the addict initially. Any assistance should be given, as a hand up that requires action and commitment on the addict's part. ***Hand-outs are off the table***.

The addict must earn everything that is given. This will be a change for everyone involved. The family may feel guilty and the addict may claim the family is being mean or unfair. They will use guilt to divide the family. But remember, your loved one's very life and the family's well-being depends on strict adherence to the plan to facilitate the addict's recovery.

This must be a Constructive Loving plan. The plan will appear tough and uncaring to the addict and even some family members. But, it is constructive love with the long term goal of saving the addict and the family. Everything is focused on our loved one getting well. Notice I did not say make the addict happy! That gift will come later.

Step one will most likely be inpatient treatment.

This is an act of commitment by the addict to show the family our addict is truly serious about recovery. They may resist this idea stating every conceivable excuse such as I will lose my job, I am in school, or a variety of illogical excuses, given the end result of continuing down this path is death or prison. There will be many more pressing issues in the addict's mind that will be an excuse for not checking into a rehabilitation center.

Remember, the addict is in fear. This fear is of withdrawal, change, and the thought of living without a chemical sense of ease and comfort. Remind the addict that whatever they think is more important will be lost due to death or jail.

Stick to the plan and withhold any, and all assistance until the addict agrees.

Even if a stay in a rehabilitation center failed in the past, it must be repeated to start the process of recovery over again. The difference is this time the family is properly armed with the education and a plan to help the addict. The family may have spent thousands of dollars for such treatment in the past, but there are low or no cost treatment facilities available and that should be an option to lessen the burden on the family.

How long should the addict's stay be in the rehabilitation center? Experience has shown that thirty days is the absolute minimum stay for effective detoxification and the initial education on how to live clean and sober. I recommend six months for optimal results.

After the agreed upon length of stay, the facility may start giving the patient privileges such as phone calls or devises such as MP3 players. Phone contact with the family is important but should be restricted to only family. This must be a hard and fast rule.

There is danger that connections with fellow addicts on the outside will hurt the chances of quality recovery. If you can control the minutes, do so. Be wary not to give the patient too much or everything they ask for. That is what they are used to getting from you in the past. Your addict must immediately see the family change.

We want to reinforce that everything is earned and that blind handouts are not going to happen. We should be comforted that the rehabilitation center gives the patient everything they need to begin recovery and return to health. Therefore, be careful not to provide items that will distract from the purpose of rehabilitation.

If they want an MP3 player, provide instead books on recovery, spirituality, or self-improvement. In all rehabilitation facilities there are opportunities for the family to visit. Do take advantage of these opportunities. This gives the family a chance to show their loved one that they care, reinforce the family plan, see how your loved one is coping, and to set a solid foundation when the patient is released.

While the loved one is in the rehabilitation center they are physically healing, taking a breath, thinking, reflecting, and learning the basic skills to stay clean and sober when they are released. This is also the family's time to do the same. The family also has the time to heal, reflect, take a deep breath, and decompress.

This is an opportunity for each family member to list everything that they did wrong in dealing with the addicted love one and share those thoughts with the family. Then have a family meeting to agree on the family's plan during the rehabilitation period and after release.

Step two is after care.

Here the family and the addict are faced with tough decisions. If the addict is an adult, they legally have the right to make the decision. The family should give recommendations. The addict must understand that the family's level of support will be based on their decision. If the loved one is a minor, their opinion should be heard but the decision is solely the parent or guardian. Here are the options available.

Half Way House (not available to minors)

These are group homes that allow the addict to transition from inpatient rehabilitation to life in the real world. The normal stay at a halfway house is generally six months to a year but could be longer. This is an opportunity for the person to become responsible for their actions and their life and stand on their own two feet. They force the addict to work and pay their own way. They are responsible for chores and like duties at the house.

As they are working to earn money for a car, the facilities often provide transportation to and from work. They have onsite recovery meetings and also transportation for the members of the house to local recovery meetings, doctor appointments, ETC. Most halfway houses are private for-profit businesses and should be researched thoroughly. Some group home halfway houses are better than others and the family can be searching for the best ones while their loved one is still in treatment.

Home with the family

This can be a dangerous course of action. The familiarity of the home setting can cause the loved one and the family to fall into old habits. The burden of getting to and from work and meetings often will fall on the family. This is a great strain on the family and gives Mr. Hyde a greater chance to manipulate the situation.

If that is the choice the family makes, strict rules must be created and enforced. Free access to transportation is dangerous because they may gravitate to old people, places, and things that are not conducive to recovery. Scheduled counseling and support group meetings must be strictly adhered to. Any violation of the rules must result in the adult to be required to leave the home.

Go back to their previous home or apartment

This is the most dangerous and least preferred choice. If the person has an established residence, they will naturally want to go home. If they have a live-in partner or spouse, they will want to reunite. Clearly they could not stay clean and sober in this environment thus this choice is fraught with danger.

If there is a partner or spouse, they would have to be 100% brought in and sold on the plan of action or, in this case, it is doomed from the start. In this case, assuming everyone in the house is on board the family still can support from their home. Frequent visits to the home will be critical. The partner or spouse cannot handle our loved one by themselves and will need the entire families support to enforce the plan.

Step three is long term after care

If we make it through the initial stage of aftercare without relapse, there is no time to declare victory. Remember, this is a lifelong mental condition that must be treated for life. The addict can quickly forget how bad it was and the hard work it took to get back on their feet. They may begin to think and feel that they have it licked based on what they have achieved from their short time in sobriety.

I have heard stories of relapse in hundreds of Alcoholics Anonymous meetings and the number one reason given for relapse is an attitude of *I got this and I don't need any more treatment.*

I never think I got this licked because I continue to go to meetings and hear the stories of those who made this mistake. If your loved one stops treatment they will miss this critical reminder and countless others. This overconfidence can also be a warning sign for relapse.

Constant encouragement and always looking for the signs of both recovery and relapse is critical for the entire family. One excellent maintenance technique is to occasionally attend counseling and support meetings with your recovering addict to show your support. Groups like Alcoholics Anonymous and Narcotics Anonymous celebrate or recognize months and then each year of clean and sober time at the meetings. This is an excellent opportunity to come a show your support.

What should we tell the loved one we are trying to save about our plan?

Everything! If you attempt to execute your plan without their knowledge, you will just confuse and anger the loved one. It is encouraged that the entire family must be present when the plan is explained to show the addict the family is all in. A frank detailed discussion of what you are willing to do to help them and what is expected from them in return is best.

Do not make threats or show anger. This is not a time for negotiation. You may even want to write it down like an agreement or contract. You may receive resistance or they may try to get you to back off on certain rules they don't like.

Do not give in. This is a one-way conversation. This is your help to give, not an entitlement they are owed. It may also be beneficial to explain how they have taken advantage of the families help in the past and the family will not make the same mistakes they made in the past. Explain the physical and emotional toll they have put you through. Explain that the old way did not work and if they desire your help, this is the one and only option available. Even if the sick loved one agrees to all the terms, expect them to test the terms early and often. The only way to stop the testing is to hold firm.

What if the loved one just plain refuses any, or all, of the family's plan of action? This is possible and be prepared for it. Do not be discouraged or give in. This means the addicted loved one just is not ready to accept the truth about their disease. Here you lay out the family's plan and how the family will help. The family emphasizes that they will be there for them when they are ready.

This is an example of constructive love. Be clear that until they are willing to follow the plan, there will be no assistance given. On this point the entire family must stand firm. This may seem harsh however, as stated earlier, the assistance given before did not help. In fact, it actually made the situation worse. It is better to not help Mr. Hyde kill your loved one by doing nothing than to help Mr. Hyde continue to kill the one you love. Be consistent and stick to the plan and ensure the family is ready when it is time.

What If, after all our Efforts, Tragedy Strikes?

The most important point I wanted to bring out in the story, The Boy in the Middle of the Lake, was that no matter what we do; efforts we take; mistakes we make, it is up to the addict to get clean and sober. This is a hard pill to swallow but it is a critical point that the entire family must accept.

The outcome rests on the addict and not the family. The good news is the family can now assist through a thorough understanding of the disease, a united family plan, and constructive love. Our illustrated story shows four different outcomes from two completely different decisions by the parents. In two of the four endings, they stepped back and in one ending, their son got better and in the other ending the son tragically died.

In the other two endings, the parents stayed their course and continued to save their son. Again, there were two different outcomes. The son died in one and the son did not in the other, but the result was the destructive misery of the parents and no recovery for the boy. It was always up to the sick addict to take the action required to get better.

What the parents did not have in the illustrated story was a thorough knowledge of the disease and agreed upon plan of action. That is why three of the four endings resulted in disaster. The family was not united and was reacting based on emotion, denial, and fear. If they had some tools to deal with the issue, they may have had a better chance in the three tragic endings. I said better chance.

We have to face the fact that, despite our best efforts, the addict may never recover. However, with a solid plan, the family does not need to be destroyed and is available and prepared to help if the opportunity avails itself. This may be of little solace to those who lose a precious loved one, but may prevent blaming each other and second-guessing ourselves.

In the communication process between the family and sick addict, this point is essential. The addict is responsible for their own life and their recovery. The family is here to help them when they decide to take their recovery seriously.

If you can take just one point from The Boy in the Middle of the Lake, I would suggest it be this:

<u>To The Family</u> - There is no one right answer and it is not your fault.

What does a person in successful long-term recovery look like?

We desperately want the person that we knew and cherished before they were plagued with this horrible and unforgiving disease back in our hearts and our lives once again. Again, here I will draw from my personal experience observing my mentors in sobriety and how I feel today about my personal growth and my sobriety.

I still want to pinch myself to ensure this is real. When a person enters recovery, success begins with observing those who have stayed sober for a long period of time. To have the ability to see these people in successful recovery, the person must finally stop lying to himself or herself that they are not that bad off. They have to look at the person in the mirror and admit that the problem is in the reflection and nowhere else.

When ready and physically and mentally present in recovery, you can now see for the first time the lives of those in successful recovery going well and they seem happy and carefree. Somehow, they have achieved what the addict may not want to admit, but desires in the depths of their being. They have recovered from this maddening condition and are no longer a slave to drugs or alcohol. They are free! If you would meet one of them for the first time, you could hardly imagine that they were ever addicted. How could they have been, they got it all together.

You immediately want what they have and realize you can have it if you are willing to put forth the effort. You, if ready, start to mimic their recipe for success, actions, attitude, and are willing to do anything to achieve that allusive solution. So, let's take a look at the recovered alcoholic and addict. The people I speak of work a continuous program of recovery, which includes meetings, working with other addicts and fellowshipping with other alcoholics and addicts.

A person who is successfully recovered from the mental obsession is a person who has been through his or her own personal hell, clawed, and climbed their way out. It is a rarity for anyone to do this alone and have the level of peace and happiness I am about to describe. The miracle of recovery is often indescribable. Every person I have observed, to include myself, was coached and mentored along the way by those who had been where each of us have been and have walked the treacherous path to sobriety.

They have a new perspective on life. Not reborn, but re-purposed and free. They are generally happy people. They have the ability to handle life's problems with an ease that inspires confidence. They realize that life's problems happen to everyone and their problems do not make them unique or persecuted.

They live a philosophy that in helping others to gain sobriety they strengthen their own sobriety. They are extremely grateful people who literally have gone from rags to being happy with the small things in life.

Yes, some find financial riches also, however, all find an intangible richness of knowing they are doing the right things on a daily basis and no longer hurting themselves or others. They went from a drain on the family and society to productive members of society. They portray a sense of peace and serenity, and that calmness is contagious to all around them.

They are no longer someone that people avoid, but are people that others rely on in crisis. They understand their own character issues and weaknesses and strive to correct their issues. They work daily to ensure they live a life that is free of resentment, fear, and anger. They stay out of other people's drama and only will intervene when asked. At that time, they will help in a loving and constructive manner. They take stock of the mistakes of the past and try to make right for those mistakes when possible.

They strive to never make those hurtful mistakes. They are extremely tough on themselves knowing that they are making up for lost time and opportunities. They fully realize that they are human and will continue to err; however, they will quickly fix these mistakes and make them right.

They live their lives with a spiritual tone. Some find spirituality through organized religion and many others find it through a personal relationship with a God of their understanding, or just an understanding that they are not the "be all and end all" but part of something larger. However, this spiritual growth is seeded and if fostered, they develop a sense of humility and begin to be selfless.

They place the needs of others forefront in their daily thoughts and actions. The only area where they are completely selfish is their recovery. They realize that they cannot be a service to the family and society unless they are working on their recovery as if their life depended on it. This is because they now realize it does!

They also realize that their disease is only in remission and know, if they lose focus, they could return to active addiction and all the pain and suffering it brings. In a way they are now better people than they could have been if they didn't fall prey to this disease of addiction. This growth out of catastrophe and illness is immeasurable.

One day, seven years into my recovery, I was trying to explain what recovery was like for me to a coworker. I couldn't describe it off the top of my head. I had so much to describe and decided to reflect.

I sat and wrote this:

My life was once a whirlwind of self-absorbed, self-inflicted bedlam. A text-book example of the "chaos theory,"

I was energy propelled outward in all directions heading nowhere, causing unintentional destruction, while achieving nominal results. With age, hard experience, and honest self-reflection, my life is becoming a seamless series of beautiful adagios, flowing ever forward; fruitful to the mind and body, like a quiet and bountiful stream. Although touched daily by the inevitable and destructive storms of

life, my reaction is no longer to fight but to weather the storm and flow ever forward. I believe this is serenity.

Frank K

April 19, 2017

Good News and Bad News

Recovery is an incredible victory for the addict and the family. They are free of the chains of addiction, and their lives become transformed from a life of slavery, misery, and isolation to a life of freedom, happiness, and inclusion into all of life's possibilities and gifts. Therefore, what could possibly be the bad news? I often say to the addicts I work with, “The good news is you’re Sober and the bad news is you’re Sober.”

I go on to explain that when they were out there in the madness of the addiction, they did not know any other way to live. They did not realize they had an incurable but treatable disease. They just dealt with their situation the best they could. They knew others got sober, but did not understand or did not want to understand how they did it. Then, sometimes in a flash and sometimes slowly, they discover the solution. Some find it through self-realization, some through fear of incarceration or death; some get ordered toward the solution through the judicial system.

No matter how they find it, there is a change in thinking about their addiction. Realizing that there actually is a successful solution and way out is a miracle. Then they start down the path to successful recovery with the desperation of a dying person. They are set free!

If the addicted person loses their focus and starts to ease

up on what got them well, a relapse can occur. If the person relapses, after being introduced to the solution, the game changes for the addict. They now cannot say they do not know what they do not know. They now know better. They have witnessed the solution beginning to work for them and they see lifelong successes in others.

Upon returning to active drinking, using, or both, they will always know that there is a solution. This can lead to dangerous depression. The struggle between Dr. Jekyll and Mr. Hyde becomes an even fiercer mental battle for the addicted person. Many recovering addicts who have relapsed during the recovery process, and have found their way back to lasting recovery, speak of what can be only described as an unimaginable nightmare.

They state the satisfaction or feeling of relief they used to get from the drug is no longer there. Instead, feelings of extreme guilt and depression become overwhelming. Many find themselves driven to suicidal thoughts. Many are dead within six months of relapse. Often the cause of death is officially pronounced as an accidental overdose or maybe a car accident.

One person close to me died as a direct result of a shootout with the police. The brutal truth we in recovery believe in our hearts is they did not die of an accidental overdose. They did not accidentally drive their car off a bridge. They did not accidentally find themselves in a shootout with police. It was a guilt driven suicide disguised as an accident, overdose or death by cop.

This is by no means a testimonial against recovery. If the addict does not recover, they will continue to live in misery and likely die years before their time. They will tear apart everyone and everything they come in contact with. This is just another hard truth that the family must be aware of and a point of discussion and reminder to the family, and the person in recovery, when they see warning signs of relapse.

Letter to Your Loved One

Consistent open and honest verbal communication is important throughout the entire recovery process. However, the interpretation of the spoken word can vary from the sender to the receiver, especially if the receiver is still in the fog of detoxification and early recovery. Memories of conversations will fade as time passes. You may consider writing your expectations down and presenting them to your loved one.

Here is an example of a letter written to a daughter in a rehabilitation center. It can be used a starting point for your own letter to start the partnership in recovery.

Our Beloved Daughter,

We love you dearly and want to help you recover from this deadly addiction. We are pleased that you are back at a rehabilitation center getting the help you need. Please use this time wisely. Starting the process of recovery should be your only focus while you are there. We have researched the disease of addiction so that we can better help you stay clean and sober when you get out.

We would like to apologize to you. We had not been properly educated on the disease of addiction and our attempts to help you may have hurt both you and us in the process. We are now better armed with the facts and will be able to better enable your recovery from this point on.

Over the past eight years, we attempted to help you with your court issues by finding you the best lawyer available, we have ensured you had a car to get to work and school, we helped with rent and utility payments when you were behind. We gave you a place to live when you were homeless. We did all of this to ensure you were not imprisoned, homeless, or dead. All of these actions were in the hope that your stated desire to become clean and sober actually would come to pass, but the addiction prevented it.

What we failed to understand was that all the help we gave was not to you at all, the person we love so dearly. The Addict that lives inside you and is trying to kill you every day stole the help. We realize that we were helping the addict kill you. You did not lie and steal from us all these years, the addict did. When you were out there drinking and using, you lost yourself and the addict took over. The addict made us sick right along with you. We will never again help the addict kill you.

Another important fact we learned was what clean

and sober really means. We thought that if you had no drugs or alcohol in your system you were clean and sober.

We now understand this deadly disease of addiction. We know that you will always suffer from the disease of addiction. There is no cure. However, the disease can be treated and you can put the disease in remission and recover from this overwhelming desire to use.

Today we wish to partner with you in your recovery. We pledge to no longer fall prey to the addict that has invaded your body and mind and has manipulated us into assisting him in hurting you.

This partnership requires you to realize that you have a disease that only can be treated by a long-term plan of recovery. If you commit to a lifelong program and put every effort into it, we will be there to help you.

If the addict inside you convinces you not to make this commitment, then we will not partner with you. We cannot and will never assist the addict again.

This commitment starts now by taking advantage of your time in this rehabilitation center. This is this initial phase of your recovery.

The real work starts when you are released. This time you will not return home. You will go to a halfway house where you will learn the tools and skills to stay clean and sober.

Here you will be expected to get and hold a job, do your part to take care of the group home, attend daily recovery meetings, and earn money to buy your own car for the first time.

Upon release from the halfway house, you must continue to treat your disease daily by attending recovery meetings. If you do your part, and we are convinced that the person we are seeing is you and not the addict, then we can begin to actively start giving you a hand up.

We will no longer give handouts. We will help you, when we can. However, you have to own your recovery.

During your recovery, you may get frustrated and feel we are not doing enough. It will take time for you to recover and until we are sure the addict living in you is in remission, we must hold back to save you from the addict inside you. It is more important that all of us do not fall back into the addict's trap.

How will we know whether we are seeing you or the addict? We have done the research to tell the difference. We will share what we learned with you over the next few weeks.

Please partner with us to banish and free you from the addict that lives inside you.

All our love,

Mom and Dad

Daily Reminders

- Addiction is a disease!

- Addiction affects both the mind and the body.

- Alcohol is a drug.

- The treatment from the mental obsession sets the addict up for real success in remaining abstinent from their drug of choice and all mind-altering substances to include legal forms like alcohol.

- The addict must never touch any brain altering substance if they want to recover.

- Do not get sick right along with the addict.

- The family cannot truly help the addict if they are sick themselves!

- Do not hate the addict, if you have to hate something, hate the disease!
- Understand the difference between your loved one (Dr. Jekyll) and the addict (Mr. Hyde).
- Do not be fooled by Mr. Hyde!
- Your loved one is a slave to the addiction.
- Do not become a slave to the addict.
- Having no drugs or alcohol in your system is not clean nor sober!
- Remember, Mr. Hyde is always there, the addict is never cured.
- Recovery is a lifelong process.
- There is no cure for the disease of addic tion.
- Addiction is treatable and treatment must last a lifetime.
- Change tough love to Constructive Love.
- This is a life and death errand for the addict and yes, the entire family.

- The family must have a plan of action.
- Communicate the plan to the addict.
- If addiction affects the entire family, then recovery becomes a family affair.
- Handouts are off the table; only give a hand up.
- Recovery is the responsibility of the addict.

Signs of Recovery

- They change their people they hang out with and replace them with more positive and productive people.

- They avoid the places and hangouts that they frequented in addiction.

- They avoid activities that fostered and encouraged drug or alcohol use.

- They are generally excited about recovery.

- They are consistent in attending treatment and do not have to be reminded to go.

- They read recovery literature and seek out recovery videos, articles, and blogs on-line.

- They begin to look better and appear healthy.
- They focus on hygiene and neatness.
- They become more responsible with money they earn.
- They may develop a sense of spirituality, which is encouraged in most twelve-step programs.
- They will become less selfish and attempt to be altruistic or selfless.
- They will start showing the ability to control their emotions and deal better with anger, rage, fear, and sadness.
- They will become more resilient and demonstrate the ability to push through setbacks.
- There is no one right answer and it is not your fault.
-They begin to make Amends.

Warning Signs for Relapse

- They begin to isolate themselves and withdraw from the family.
- They begin to become too busy to go to meetings or counseling.
- They begin to reconnect with associates they knew in active addiction.
- They feel the need to visit the bars or the parties where the primary focus is drinking or drug use.
- Other priorities replace the excitement for their program of recovery.
- They begin to act out and show less patience.
- They start having trouble meeting their financial obligations.

- They begin to ask to borrow money with increased frequency.
- Their routines change.
- They become secretive and become increasingly annoyed with inquiries about how they are doing.
- Their physical appearance and hygiene begins to change.
- They show an inability to take care of simple things like household cleaning, and laundry.
- They decide they no longer need treatment or meetings.

Final Thoughts

Recovery is an incredible victory for the addict and the family. But despite our best efforts, it is up to the addicted person to accept the treatment and work their recovery on a daily basis. This is a hard pill for a mother, father, brother, sister, husband, wife, son, or daughter to swallow. Remember, I said there is no magic pill we can give our loved one to make it all better.

We can only set the conditions for the addict to recover. We do this by understanding the disease of addiction. We must fully realize that this is both a mental and physical disease and attack it with that mindset. We must realize that the addicted is always being tested by the addict inside (Mr. Hyde) and must guard against being manipulated by that alter ego. We must encourage, expect, and witness a commitment to lifelong treatment from the addict before we freely help them. Trust, but verify, is our watchword. We must be open and honest with our addict and the family must act as a team and not stray from the plan of action.

The bulleted daily reminders, signs of recovery, and warning signs for relapse should be reviewed often to ensure the family does not become complacent. Periodic family meetings to review how the plan is working can also be helpful.

Finally, the family cannot get sick right along with the addict. If the addict is ready to recover and we are too broken and sick ourselves, we may lose the opportunity that we have dreamed about.

Our Illustrator
A Self Portrait

Holly West is a rising sophomore at Willmar High School in Willmar, Minnesota. Her favorite subjects are history, English, and art.

She hopes to expand her artistic abilities after high school, and this project was a way to turn a hobby into something more rewarding. She plans to attend college and pursue a degree in graphic design and visual arts.

A cut out for the mirror or refrigerator

Daily Reminders

Addiction is a disease!
Addiction affects both the mind and the body.
Alcohol is a drug.
The treatment from the mental obsession sets the addict up for real success in remaining abstinent from their drug of choice and all mind altering substances to include legal forms like alcohol.
The addict must never touch any brain altering substance if they want to recover.
Do not get sick right along with the addict.
The family cannot truly help the addict if they are sick themselves!
Do not hate the addict, if you have to hate something, hate the disease!
Understand the difference between your loved one (Dr. Jekyll) and the addict (Mr. Hyde).
Do not be fooled by Mr. Hyde!
Your loved one is a slave to the addiction.
Do not become a slave to the addict.
Having no drugs or alcohol in your system is not clean nor sober!
Remember, Mr. Hyde is always there, the addict is never cured.
Recovery is a lifelong process.
There is no cure for the disease of addiction.
Addiction is treatable and treatment must last a lifetime.
Change tough love to Constructive Love.
This is life and death errand for the addict and yes, the entire family.
The family must have a plan of action.
Communicate the plan to the addict.
If addiction affects the entire family, then recovery becomes a family affair.
Handouts are off the table; only give a hand up.
Recovery is the responsibility of the addict

www.ingramcontent.com/pod-product-compliance
Lightning Source LLC
LaVergne TN
LVHW051234080426
835513LV00016B/1576

* 9 7 8 1 9 3 7 5 0 8 6 2 3 *